Ning Duty Free Art, Hito Steyerl Hyper-
y Morton Everything, David OReilly Stony
k, Theaster Gates Dark Matter Labs, Indy
sscalar Architecture of COVID-19, Ivan
ra and Andrés Jaque Space Enabled,
Tapis Rouge, Emergent Vernacular Archi-
cia Auditorium and Congress Center,
uincho Tía Coral, Gabinete de Arquitec-
rangers, Andrés Jaque / Office for Political
koko Floating School, NLÉ Aerial Domes-
Fab and Alejandro Haiek New Andean
Freddy Mamani The Last Moments, Avril
al Park, Philippe Rahm architectes In the
am Young Color(ed) Theory, Amanda Wil-
lt of Life and Knowledge, Mass Studies
C Marching On, Bryony Roberts, Mabel
he Marching Cobras of New York CLIMA-
Zones, Cooking Sections Of Oil and Ice,
eitz MOCCA, Heatherwick Studio NAVE,
National Museum of African American
lture, Adjaye Associates Ocho Quebradas
tal Lycée Schorge, Kéré Architecture Fuy-
mplex, Amateur Architecture Studio Polis
Gang Palestinian Museum, Heneghan
p Water Garden, Junya Ishigami + Asso-
ouf Mosque, Marina Tabassum CopenHill,
mmuter Train, Kazuyo Sejima & Associates
Opera, Diller Scofidio + Renfro THREAD:
ency and Cultural Center, Toshiko Mori
es of Transformation, Lacaton & Vassal,
t, and Karine Dana Housing +, Tatiana
nzolco Cultural Center, Isaac Broid and
arling Site Museum and entrance, Valerio
d Forest for the Trojan Women, Stefano
Feedlots, Mishka Henner The Proposal,
L, eon (I, II), Julie Mehretu Moriyama-San,

Bêka
John
Asia
gang
Michael Rakowitz Love is
is Death, Arthur Jafa Black
Year 3, Steve McQueen A F
Institute of Isolation, Luc
Orchestra, Bernie Krause ar
Religious and Secular Co
Studio Chahar A Songyang
Pavilion, Frida Escobedo V
Z33 new wing, Francesca
Granby Four Streets, Assen
Hasegawa Flat House, Pr
Village — Smallacre City, D
Structures of Landscape, Er
Neighborhood Developme
Bamboo Hostels, Anna Heri
WORKac New Dark Age,
Kahiu X-Ray Architecture, B
away: Story Telling for Earth
Anatomy of an AI System,
Joler Forensic Architecture
the Underground, Nelly Be
Commune, Ou Ning Duty
objects, Timothy Morton Ev
Island Arts Bank, Theaster (
Johar The Transscalar Arc
Lopez Munuera and And
Danielle Wood Tapis Rouge
tecture Plasencia Auditor
SelgasCano Quincho Tía (
tura Intimate Strangers, An
Innovation Makoko Floatin
ticity, Lab.Pro.Fab and Ale

Radical Architecture of the Future

beatrice
galilee

radical architecture of the future

Architecture's Radical Future 6

visionaries
insiders
radicals
breakthroughs
masterminds

Further Reading 230
Index 232

ns
s

12
58
122
158
196

Architecture's Radical Future

> It matters what thoughts think thoughts.
> It matters what worlds world worlds.
> It matters what stories tell stories.
>
> Donna Haraway, *Staying with the Trouble: Making Kin in the Chthulucene*

Long before the visitors arrive to the museum, busily removing their jackets and unfolding their maps; before staff start to crisscross their way across great halls, hurrying past masterpieces to get to their early morning meetings; before the security teams huddle and then disperse to assume their positions, there is a time to see things alone. I am by no means an early bird, but during five years working at the Metropolitan Museum of Art (Met) in New York as its curator of architecture and design,[1] I found these quiet moments allowed me to reflect on the myriad ways architecture is presented within the museum. Architecture, an extreme and evocative endeavor of our species, is not only present in the collection displays of almost every one of the museum's departments — which together span the history of more than five thousand years of human culture — it is also often the major attraction.

The Ancient Near East galleries tell a story of the beginning of human civilization through vivid fragments of polychrome glazed and inscribed bricks recovered from the ancient Mesopotamian city of Babylon; in the Department of Egyptian Art, a temple, displaced from its sandy site of Dendur, was removed and reconstructed stone by etched-upon stone in a glazed courtyard with a reflecting pool. The entrance to the American Wing is marked by a vast courtyard with one wall clad in the neoclassical facade of a nineteenth-century Wall Street bank — the historic roots of its tightly coiled Ionic columns and porticos can be seen on display a short walk away in the Met's expansive collection of marble antiquities. In the galleries showing the cultures of Oceania, columns, house posts and other artifacts speak to the symbolism of thresholds and the timeless universality of using architecture to convey power and wealth.

The action of building and development, as Colombian anthropologist Arturo Escobar suggests, can no longer be left unquestioned. In his book *Designs for the Pluriverse: Radical Interdependence, Autonomy, and the Making of Worlds* (2018), he advocates creating worlds within worlds, each responding to the complexities of the relationships between the northern and southern hemispheres. "There is no doubt that after decades of what has been called 'development,' the world is in crisis — systemic, multiple, and asymmetrical; long in the making, it now extends across all continents," he writes. "Never before did so many crucial aspects of life fail simultaneously, and people's expectations for their own and children's futures look so uncertain. Crisis manifestations are felt across all domains: environmental, economic, social, political, ethical, cultural, spiritual, and embodied."[2] The work of the myriad practitioners in these pages is not only geared to designing for the future, but also seeks to mitigate against it by advocacy work that introduces sustainable new methodologies or by finding alternatives to construction altogether.

Much of the DNA of this group is shared with the roots of the 1960s and 1970s avant-garde. They were also captivated by the promise of technology and outer space, concerned by environmentalism and civil rights — now as then there is a call to remake the social order. But now these topics and issues are supercharged; they are interconnected, electrified, and global.

When compiling this array of diverse projects, one thing that became clear is that the terms under which architecture exists today — permanent, patriarchal, capitalistic, upholding a Western canon — have changed. The biggest civil rights movement of a generation, Black Lives Matter, which took place over the summer of 2020 has precipitated much-needed reflection on the role of architects in manifesting an unjust social order of largely white male privilege, as well as the discipline's explicit contribution to the planet's ecological catastrophe.

These ephemeral and nontraditional forms of spatial practices — from the worlds of science-fiction set design to street performances, drones to outdoor operas — are complex, meaningful, and fascinating. Just as the artist Michael Rakowitz (see p. 144) recreated an ancient lamassu sculpture — most of which have been removed from their sites in the Middle East and placed in museum collections — in London's Trafalgar Square and told through its materiality a poignant history of Iraq. In this book, as in my curatorial practice, which includes experimental biennales, conferences, and performances, I use architecture as a means to allow me to go beyond the physical form and into the complex and contradictory histories, from the personal to public, the humble to grandiose.

The seventy-nine projects included in this book are completed projects. They are the precedents, case studies, and inspirations of a diversified, conscientious, nimble, and responsive future architecture. There is no single aesthetic or political consensus that unites the practitioners, though there are affinities and allegiances between many of their forms of practice. These alliances are explored in five chapters: "Visionaries," "Insiders," "Radicals," "Breakthroughs," and "Masterminds." "Visionaries" are architects who have diversified their practices, finding alternative ways of exploring space apart from or in addition to the act of building, such as Andrés Jaque (see pp. 24–25 and 223), Philippe Rahm (see pp. 36–39), and Amanda Williams (see pp. 42–43). The "insiders" are often household name architecture firms, such as Diller Scofidio + Renfro (see pp. 102–105) or Adjaye Associates (see pp. 66–69), whose eminence becomes the key to experiment or push against the status quo. The multifaceted, multihyphenated "radical" practitioners are those artists whose images — including Mishka Henner's *Feedlots* series (see pp. 124–27) and Arthur Jafa's video work *Love is the Message, The Message is Death* (see p. 145) — shatter expectations and linger long in the mind. "Breakthroughs" are new voices whose stars are still rising, whether in the built environment, like New York-based SO – IL (see pp. 174–75), or through image-making, like Beijing's Drawing Architecture Studio (see pp. 180–81). The "masterminds" are those like Timothy Morton (see p. 217) and Indy Johar (see p. 222), whose cross-pollination of ideas across many disciplines is a fundamental aspect of the culture and machinations of contemporary architectural production. The fluid nature of these practitioners means that they could easily belong in one or more of these categories.

Indeed, the idea of the future itself is being questioned by this generation of radical thinkers and makers. As Donna Haraway (see pp. 202–203) writes in her essay "A Cyborg Manifesto" (1985): "The boundary between science fiction and social reality is an optical illusion."[3] The most chilling and unimaginable stories of recent years have come from global news reports. In the space of a less than a year, a funeral was held for a Swiss glacier,[4] close to a billion animals were estimated to have been killed in infernos across Australia, scientists announced that half of all insects on Earth are expected to be extinct within fifty years, and all within a hundred,[5] and among the many unprecedented consequences of the coronavirus pandemic was that demand for oil dropped so radically that on some days its value on the stock market was negative—costing traders to sell it—at minus thirty-seven dollars a barrel.[6]

Much of the work of practitioners in this book occupies space that oscillates between science fiction and science fact. To paraphrase the artist and academic Hito Steyerl (see p. 216), the hybrid digital-physical nature of much of the world today is extremely strange, and people's inability to differentiate between the two is stranger still. The gripping hyperreality of CGI has led to a paucity of imagination elsewhere—robotics designers are hiring the digital artists who conceive fictional robots for movies,[7] and the US Army has been advertising on game streaming websites, using the platforms as a recruitment tool.[8] These uncanny situations are examined in academic and science-fiction artist and architect Liam Young's practice (see pp. 40–41), which explores the relationship between Hollywood fantasy and real-world design, culminating in the creation of his studio course Fictions and Entertainment at SCI-Arc university in Los Angeles. His premise is that most people's perception of the world is shaped and informed by mediums of fiction, from TV to cinema, video games, and the constructed, confirmation bias-filled narratives of the news. Young's film *In the Robot Skies* is set in a nearby universe, rather than a future one.

Both Steyerl and Young join James Bridle (see p. 198) and Kate Crawford and Vladan Joler (see pp. 204–205) in noting that a new type of radical architecture is emerging that is not designed for humans—it consists of vast, sprawling data centers housing service routers, underwater pipes, and servers that make up the physical infrastructure of the internet. The work of the AI Now Institute's Anatomy of an AI System is Crawford and her team's efforts to pin down, and make graphic, the exact kind and quantities of human and material labor involved in the making and functioning of a single Amazon Alexa home assistant. The astonishing resulting large-scale graphic map was installed across an entire wall at *Broken Nature: Design Takes on Human Survival*, an exhibition curated by Paola Antonelli as part of the Milan Triennial in 2019. Also in that exhibition was *The Great Animal Orchestra* (see pp. 156–57), a site-specific installation by Bernie Krause and United Visual Artists that uses detailed layers of sound to recall the spaces and species that—at that time, at least—were living and thriving in an Amazonian rainforest.

Antonelli remarks in the exhibition catalog that: "Design should be centred not only on humans but on the future of the whole biosphere as well. Its approaches should aim not only to correct humanity's self-destructive course but also to replenish our relationship with all environments and all species — including other human beings."[9] At a scale of weather patterns, atmosphere, geology, and land use, the path that nature has taken is the one that humans have charted. This anthropogenic focus of design is not limited to what reads easily as human made, as Beatriz Colomina (see pp. 200–201) writes in the catalog for the 2016 exhibition *Are We Human?*: "The apparent lack of design in vast parts of the world — the Arctic, the Amazon, the desert, the oceans, the atmosphere — is a mirage, a deadly effect. Inequalities are being crafted in everything we see, don't see or don't want to see."[10] The practitioners included in this book share those values, using architecture as an agent of change, often collaborating with or railing against government forces and local groups.

Interrogating and rethinking global chains of supply for the building industry is fundamental to the work of architects here. Many projects in this book are by architects who made the decision to innovate using a limited palette of three or four materials unique to the existing context. Projects by Marina Tabassum (see pp. 90–93), Gabinete de Arquitectura (see pp. 22–23), Toshiko Mori (see pp. 106–109), and Kéré Architecture (see pp. 74–77) are among these. Other firms, including Practice Architecture (see pp. 178–79), Lacaton & Vassal (see pp. 110–11), and Rotor DC (see pp. 46–47), take an active role in campaigning for and integrating adaptive reuse and low embodied carbon. In the case of Japanese architect Junya Ishigami (see pp. 86–89), the architect went to extreme lengths to preserve a small forest by uprooting it and moving it to an adjacent plot.

These issues draw from currents of thought that originally emerged in the second half of the twentieth century when radical architects began to react against international Modernism, concerned, as architects are today, with what was a universal, European exceptionalism. The term *critical regionalism* was coined as a way to position architecture against the prefabrication and homogenizing forces of capitalism and consumer culture. At the Museum of Modern Art in New York, Bernard Rudofsky's influential 1964 exhibition *Architecture Without Architects* explored global forms of vernacular architecture in a time when copying classical designs for every institutional building — from train stations to banks — had only recently fallen out of style. In the preface to the catalog, he writes: "Architectural history, as written and taught in the Western world has never been concerned with more than a few select cultures. In terms of space it comprises but a small part of the globe — Europe, stretches of Egypt and Anatolia or little more than was known in the second century AD"[11] Rudofsky saw an opportunity to turn to the elementals of building, offering an alternative to the elitist Western narrative of architectural history.

More than half a century has passed since Rudofsky's exhibition, and it is evident that colonial legacies still endure, and his statement is just as valid now. The radical thinkers and leaders in the profession included in this book are involved in decolonizing architectural strategies in order to return to the roots and culture of the places they live. The work of Sweet Water Foundation (see pp. 186–87) and Amanda Williams draws attention to systemic racism in the United States, when cities were racially segregated by planners, and loans and investment was refused to predominantly Black neighborhoods, the system known as redlining. Picket fences once symbolized an "American dream" of wealthy, happy suburbia that the States exported to the world, but the reality is that the government mandate for Levittown, the first mass-produced suburb of America, was that no Black families were allowed to live there.

Much of the radical architecture of the twentieth century was conceived in the animated political and social context of the 1960s and 1970s. Space exploration, nuclear power, radical individualism, and civil rights movements led to an atmosphere of potentially great and meaningful change in the world. In Japan, the constructions of the Metabolists—a group of architects chiefly led by Kenzo Tange, who designed interconnected master plans for Japanese cities and major buildings globally—were extraordinary prefabricated concrete megastructures, created in the wake of the scorched earth of World War II. The group described their designs as *metabolistic*, with master plans that were not fixed, because they expected the modular cells of the city—the buildings and highways—to grow freely and informally. In Europe other radicals, including Dutch artist Constant Nieuwenhuys and Hungarian-born French architect Yona Friedman, created stunning drawings of megastructures and cities, visions of new ways people might live, work, and travel. Just as the radical architects included in this book are influenced by contemporary thinkers, the designers of the 1960s worked often in tandem with philosophers and theorists, such as Georges Bataille, Guy Debord, and Ivan Chtcheglov. Similarly, the witty pop culture references and sense of enthusiasm and wonder for the modern world, evident in Archigram's imaginative multiverses of walking cities and flying buildings, and the inflatable and psychedelic buildings of Ant Farm, stemmed from their fascination with space capsules, the Atomic Age, the culture of fast food and mass production, and the promise of computers.

Throughout the twentieth century, many cities in Latin America rebuilt themselves under Modernism, even as Latin America's natural resources — "open veins"[12] — were all but run dry through the previous centuries of colonial rule. The region took the lead in radical form making, with projects such as Oscar Niemeyer's design of an entire city that rejected the rectilinear traditions of the West, instead featuring grand, fluid spaces. Other standouts include Mexican-Spanish architect Félix Candela's elegant concrete hyperbolic-parabola engineering and Uruguayan architect-engineer Eladio Dieste's beautiful all-brick curving structures. In Brazil, Lina Bo Bardi's manifestos on refuse and public space, and her own high profile as a writer, designer, and illustrator, stood out among the few female architects working in the public realm at that time.[13] Radical architecture then and now is connected by a sense of disenfranchisement.

Yet the canon as it stands is being rewritten. Topics of race and colonialism are finally entering contemporary architectural history books, and in Latin America and across Africa and the global south, architects, urban planners, and engineers, as well as a global diaspora of migrants are resisting and questioning the modus operandi of contributing to a universal Western canon of building. This book seeks to contribute to this new condition: holding up work that offers new thoughts and challenges expectations, and pushing new, complex, and dissonant voices into the mainstream.

In 2017, as part of my research as curator of Argentinian sculptor Adrián Villar Rojas' exhibition *The Theater of Disappearance*,[14] which was staged on the roof of the Met, I found myself late one night in the Department of Egyptian Art, standing in front of tiny wooden models discovered by the museum's archeologists at the turn of the twentieth century. The maquettes, some of them four thousand years old, portray farms, walls, houses, and gardens. One of them was so perfectly preserved that the columns that hold up the portico still show the vivid patterns and bright hieroglyphics that would have been evident in the colorful architecture of many of the cities of antiquity. The architecture of the future — often immaterial; traversing media, social structures, and liminal spaces; and made by people who may not identify as architects or designers — might not be as easy to preserve or to study as the Egyptian maquettes, but it suggests a similarly polychromatic outlook. It is an active contribution to a more expansive and multi-layered narrative, one that is open-ended, multiple, and in continuous evolution.

visionaries

The visionaries in this chapter find ways to positively transform spaces by using unconventional and multifaceted techniques. These practitioners — architects and otherwise — identify the complex needs and wants of individuals or communities, and integrate them into their design process. They welcome the variety of ways in which architecture can contribute to a society without building. For example, designers and researchers collaborate with a drumline and dance team to provide visibility to cultural traditions; an architect alters the density of air in a public park as a response to a humid climate; and the indigenous heritage of a city is reinstituted through the colors and forms of a body of built works. Elsewhere, an office usually celebrated for its buildings and installations has created an in-depth study of digital forms of representation and activism in LGBTQ communities. We meet the academics and architects utilizing the feedback loops between science fiction and real life to explore radical solutions to climate change and envision applications of near-future technologies. Various studios seeking to address problems such as the climate crisis, the harmful impacts of industrial ocean farming, wasteful material supply chains, and urban blight have created new business models or artistic interventions as a way to offer practical solutions. Those operating outside the traditional realm of architecture set a new standard for how architectural training, when connected with other disciplines, could be applied to have a deeper impact on society. In this chapter, architecture plays a fascinating role, not as a finite structure, but as an interconnective matter that flows between the reality and potential of social spaces, individual lives, and materials.

Tapis Rouge, Emergent Vernacular Architecture
Port-au-Prince, Haiti, 2016

After a devastating 2010 earthquake in Haiti, teams of non-profits including the American Red Cross began to formulate plans to rebuild and heal the affected areas. On a site in a neighborhood mostly composed of densely knit, informal housing in the capital Port-au-Prince, London– and Port-au-Prince–based research and design practice Emergent Vernacular Architecture devised a project that consists of a public amphitheater and gathering space. Tapis Rouge's concentric rings serve to define separate amenities for the community, including exercise equipment, seating, and a water distribution station that brings well water to the surface from 328 ft. (100 m) below ground. On a perimeter wall is a mural painted by local artists and residents. Unlike a traditional process in which designers present a finished project, they worked in tandem with locals throughout, using a series of participatory design exercises and workshops. This was not only because it is an ethical way of working, but also because the project required both physical and emotional renewal for the traumatized community postdisaster. The public space became a place where a sense of civic pride among the locals could grow. Much of EVA Studio's work takes place in Haiti and Lebanon. In the latter they have recently begun working with displaced communities of Syrian refugees, using economical and thoughtful people-first design skills to make a big impact.

1   A retaining wall, at right, was painted by local artists and residents with a colorful mural.
2   Tapis Rouge includes shared amenities for the community to use, including a set of exercise equipment.
3   Aerial view of the informal settlement, which was devastated by a 2010 earthquake. Tapis Rouge's disk-shaped form can be seen in the center.

Plasencia Auditorium and Congress Center, SelgasCano
Plasencia, Spain, 2017

1   The Plasencia Auditorium and Congress Center is wrapped in a translucent skin that allows light to enter the building's interior.

Plasencia Auditorium and Congress Center, SelgasCano
Plasencia, Spain, 2017

2 Access to the Plasencia Auditorium and Congress Center is via a vibrant orange gangway.
3 Almost invisible during the day, the building's outline starts to take shape against the sky as dusk falls.
4 The structure is designed to minimize its footprint in its arid environment.

On the perimeter of the Spanish city of Plasencia, an undefinable form, seemingly part chrysalis, part meteorite, glows from the inside. Conceived by Spanish architecture firm SelgasCano, this extraordinary luminous center was designed by wrapping all of the functions of a theater, a dance hall, an exhibition space, and conference auditoriums into a tight ball, and then balancing that volume as lightly as possible on the existing landscape. Every aspect of the architecture is designed to make a minimal footprint on the rocky topography; the building has a volume of 86,000 sq. ft. (8,000 m²), but only 4,300 sq. ft. (400 m²) makes contact with the ground. The building is wrapped fully in a translucent skin made of the material ETFE. This durable, air-filled plastic is self-cleaning and easy to install, and it barely adds any weight to the steel-and-concrete structure. The material also offers up to a 45 percent reduction in solar heat gain, which in the hot climate of western Spain greatly reduces the financial and ecological burden of air-conditioning. Everywhere possible, unpretentious industrial and affordable materials are used in ingenious ways: a pipe duct operates as seating; a raw concrete wall was cast with a corrugated texture and painted white. At the heart of the building is a 39-ft.-deep (12 m) vertical canyon, which is linked to ramps and spiral staircases for circulation throughout the building. At night, the glowing structure is a beacon for Plasencia.

Plasencia Auditorium and Congress Center, SelgasCano
Plasencia, Spain, 2017

5   Circulation routes that wrap around the interior perimeter of the space offer panoramic views of the countryside.
6   The main auditorium has a retrofuturistic feel. Its red-toned lower half emphasizes that this is the heart of the building.
7   Playful shapes and pops of color abound in the center, changing from shades of yellow to red as the spaces move from public to private.
8   Circular apertures, bubblegum-pink rubber floors, and transparent orange walls can be found throughout public areas.

Visionaries 21

Quincho Tía Coral, Gabinete de Arquitectura
Asunción, Paraguay, 2017

Asunción, Paraguay-based architecture studio Gabinete de Arquitectura, composed of Gloria Cabral, Solano Benítez and Solanito Benítez, is known for experimental buildings that reimagine the role of brick in contemporary design. The studio has perfected nearly every possible application of the material. By experimenting with the creative capacity of brick, as well as other simple and affordable materials, the office has made a meaningful difference in often-underserved communities. On the outskirts of Asunción, the team worked on a project close to home. In the backyard of a family member, the studio constructed Quincho Tía Coral, a dramatic triangular brick-and-concrete pergola that spans the garden and runs adjacent to an outdoor pool, creating a shady canopy for barbecues. The main three-story truss-like structure is made from crushed brick rubble, rescued from a nearby brickyard, and recycled glass, all embedded into rough-hewn concrete. Integrating the found materials had the effect of creating a low-cost terrazzo. A supporting wall that wraps the perimeter of the project consists of a network of wavelike brick screens, constructed so that these bricks are turned, making an otherwise precarious system stable. Working with affordable, reclaimed materials and employing simple techniques means the firm can engage unskilled labor, in turn distributing money to the local communities.

1 The dramatic three-tier brick-and-concrete pergola spans the garden and extends alongside the pool. It is supported by an inverted V-shaped pillar.
2 A triangular motif is a recurring feature of the design.
3 The canopy provides an abundance of poolside shade.

Visionaries

Intimate Strangers, Andrés Jaque / Office for Political Innovation
2016

Based in New York and Madrid, the Office for Political Innovation's practice encompasses academic research, construction, short films, performances, and installations grounded in an overarching inquiry into the politics of space. Founder Andrés Jaque argues that architecture is never a finished product; it can only be understood by examining and decoding the shifting relationship design has with its context — a reading of its function and symbols will inevitably change with time. In preparation for creating the video installation *Intimate Strangers* — comprising multiple full-scale screens and layered audio recordings — the studio produced an urban study of Grindr, a location-based online dating app for gay, bi, trans, and queer people, reflecting on how online platforms are now being politicized. The research reveals that traditional community spaces of LGBTQ emancipation, such as clubs and bars, have been replaced by one-to-one connections in domestic spaces, produced by the technological mediation of Grindr. Geo-tagging of hookups in New York shows hot spots around areas with rising rents, suggesting Grindr use as a possible metric for future gentrification. Charting the exceptional growth of the platform — which now counts ten million users in 192 countries — the research also shows how the app is used by police in authoritarian regimes to target gay people, and how it has been mobilized as a tool by LGBTQ refugees seeking safe passage to Europe.

1   Video stills from *Intimate Strangers*, a multimedia installation in the *Fear and Love: Reactions to a Complex World* exhibition at the Design Museum in London, 2016.
2   Grindr's GPS location basis has been utilized in countries where same-sex sex is banned to track, harass, and arrest users.
3   Reenactment of a Grindr-mediated interaction.
4   Dating apps — including Grindr, Tinder, and happn — use proximity to locate potential sex partners. Some users hack their locations to access more profiles.

2

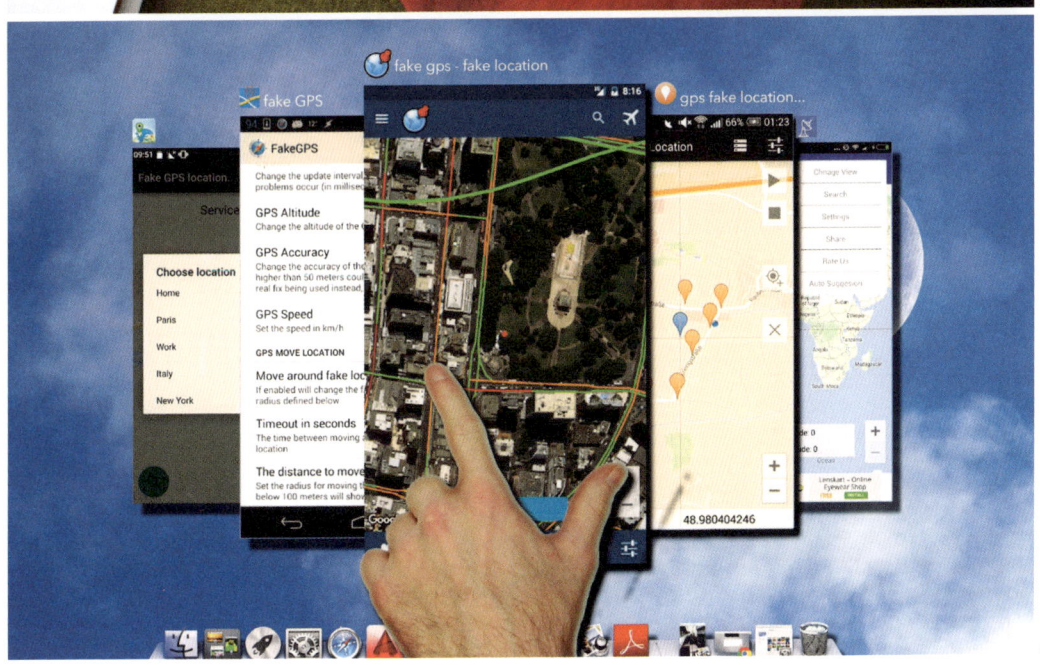

3

4

25

Makoko Floating School, NLÉ
Lagos Lagoon, Nigeria, 2016

On a lagoon in the heart of Nigeria's largest city, Lagos, the inhabitants of the neighborhood of Makoko are used to living with water. But global warming, rising sea levels, and extreme poverty have forever transformed ways of living in the coastal settlement. Most Makoko residents fashion their homes on precariously floating pontoons, moving through their neighborhood on canoes. Local children have often been without somewhere to go to school. After visiting the area, Lagos– and Amsterdam–based architect Kunlé Adeyemi designed and built the experimental Makoko Floating School as an educational space for the next generation of Makoko residents. Using a large A-frame shape with a low center of gravity (a floating ballast made of 250 recycled water barrels), the entire three-story structure was constructed with nothing more complicated than a hand drill. The ground floor provided space where children could play and community members could gather, and two upper floors housed classrooms. The bright blue roof became a symbol of investment in this neglected part of the city. Sadly, the structure eventually collapsed following heavy rains in 2015, and only briefly served as a school. However, the project demonstrated how to create a new form of urbanism within the context of a highly dense environment and has spurred ongoing research by the studio into ways in which humans can coexist with land and water, including new iterations in Italy and China.

1 The completed school floats on a lagoon in the Makoko neighborhood of Lagos, Nigeria.
2 The temporary A-frame structure was assembled using wooden beams on top of a ballast made from 250 recycled water barrels.
3 A third iteration of the Makoko Floating School on the Jincheng Lake in the city of Chengdu, China in 2018.

Visionaries

Aerial Domesticity, Lab.Pro.Fab and Alejandro Haiek
Mexico City, Mexico, 2018

Lab.Pro.Fab is an international research, urban design, and architecture studio that is fascinated by the infrastructural ecosystems that operate between design, architecture, and the city. With projects that range from performances to large-scale public buildings and urban infrastructure, the office reconciles the material excesses of industrial manufacturing — the waste produced by construction — with social and civic deficits, including unrest, poverty, and inequality. In a temporary project for a festival in Mexico City, the team deconstructed a typical Latin American residence and separated each room into one of several small transparent pods, each situated on the top of a cherry picker in an urban square. The architects wanted to draw attention to the dimensions and physical constraints of the domestic spaces that most people endure in mass housing, while also revealing some elements of the hardware of architectural production. The materials of the installation all came from the construction industry, with many of the household items sourced secondhand from Craigslist. The work straddles art, architecture, design, engineering, and performance — the pods being occupied and mobilized during the festival.

1   As part of the Mextropoli Festival, *Aerial Domesticity* took over a public square in Mexico City.
2   The project reconstructed domestic spaces through a series of cherry pickers, inhabited over a three-day period.
3   Each cherry picker was fitted with a transparent cocoon — made in collaboration with Mexico City–based construction firm Manada — which was fabricated out of polycarbonate off-cuts.
4   The activities of daily life, such as reading and relaxing, were removed from their usual domestic contexts and performed in the public sphere.

1

2

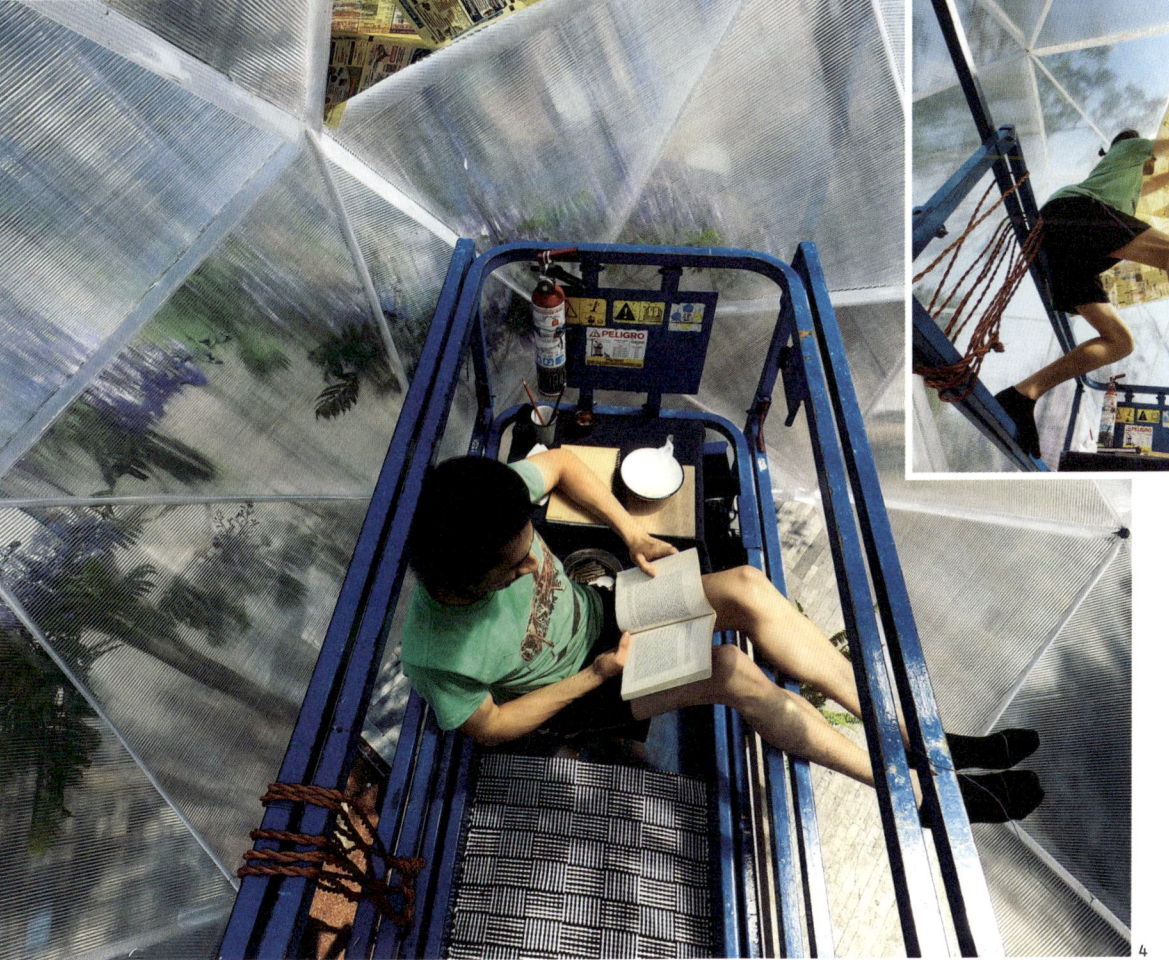

3

4

New Andean Architecture, Freddy Mamani
El Alto, Bolivia, 2005–

Born in the Aymara village of Catavi, in Bolivia, engineer turned architect Freddy Mamani's sensational technicolor buildings and interiors have become so synonymous with his adopted city of El Alto that local shops now sell miniature make-your-own Freddy Mamani buildings to tourists. His designs are deeply rooted in the heritage, textures, and traditional colors and imagery of his native Aymara people, a historically oppressed indigenous ethnic group that makes up about 25 percent of Bolivia's population. He advocates for an architecture embedded in the visual history of Tiahuanaco, an ancient imperial capital on the shores of lake Titicaca. Mamani's work in El Alto began with the design of a bold *salón de eventos* (party hall). An unusual design typology is particular to this type of building, which is funded by community-organized microloans. The ground floor is a commercial unit usually rented out to local shops; the middle is a double-height room for parties, weddings, and community festivities; and above are private apartments. This top floor often features a pitched roof and a totally different facade treatment. Through his visionary designs and advocacy for his indigenous community, Mamani has played a vital role in transforming El Alto, once a struggling, low-income settlement, into a now-thriving city of about one million people, more than three-quarters of whom are of Aymaran heritage.

1   A block with three *salónes de eventos* all designed by Freddy Mamani in El Alto, Bolivia.
2   Each project follows a similar typology with rentable commercial spaces on the ground floor, middle floors for parties and weddings, and a top-floor penthouse where the owner of the building typically lives.
3   The city of El Alto, which is close to the Andes mountains, has become synonymous with Mamani's signature style inspired by Tiahuanaco traditions and motifs.

Visionaries

New Andean Architecture, Freddy Mamani
El Alto, Bolivia, 2005–

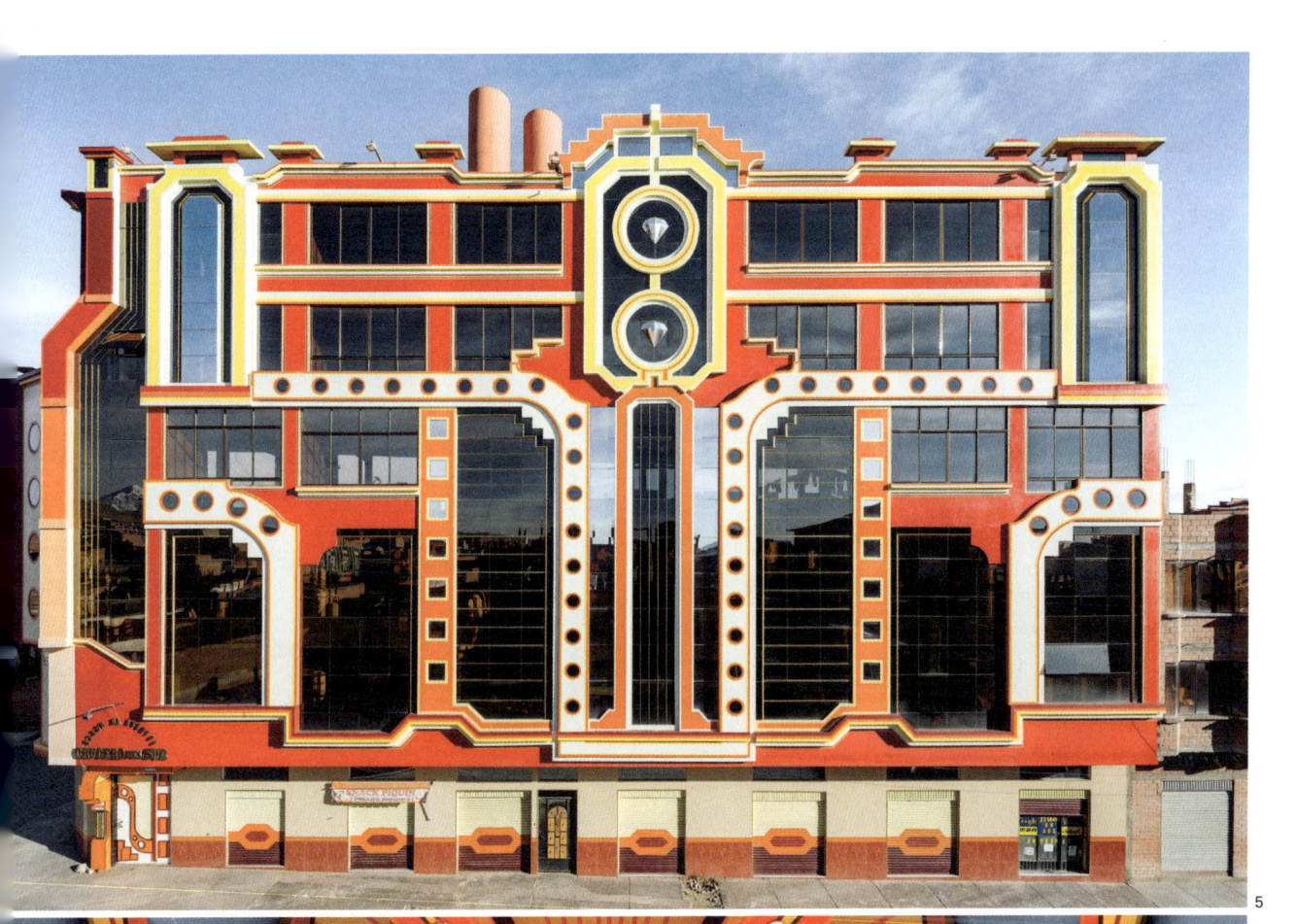

4   Mamani uses colors inspired by traditional textiles of the region, which often mix bright complementary hues.
5   The Andean cross and circle are recurring shapes in doors and windows.
6   Floral motifs form ceiling plates for modern chandeliers.

Visionaries

The Last Moments, Avril Furness
2016

What would it be like to watch your last moments? How would you feel looking at the last place you'd ever see? London-based Avril Furness's *The Last Moments* sets out to answer those questions. The virtual reality 360-degree film gives its viewers an insight into the experience of an assisted suicide. It was shot in a replica of a room at a Swiss Dignitas clinic, one of the few places in the world that offers assisted suicide. Attending an exhibition, Furness has described herself as being spellbound encountering a scale reproduction of a clinic that ends lives — she was struck particularly by how ordinary the room was.[1] She started to research testimonials from people who had made the decision to end their lives by euthanasia. Furness saw the potential of VR to document and share the complexity and compassion of the end-of-life experience and to demystify this taboo topic, including showing the medical environments designed for palliative care. The replica room was realized in concert with set designers from theater company Punchdrunk, who created an authentic-looking scene with tablecloths, cups of tea, and Swiss chocolates that replicated ones seen at Dignitas. To achieve a realistic sound experience, Furness worked with a binaural sound designer who created omnidirectional sound — if you turn your head in the film, the sound will be relative to the direction in which you're looking.

1   A scene from *The Last Moments*, showing a replica of a room at a Swiss Dignitas clinic.
2   The interactive docudrama VR film places viewers inside the room, allowing them to experience an assisted suicide for themselves.
3   The film allows for viewers' opinions to be polled, with the intention to help spark debate on this sensitive issue.

Central Park, Philippe Rahm architectes
Taichung, Taiwan, 2020

1 Conceived in collaboration with landscape architects Mosbach paysagistes and local studio Ricky Liu & Associates, Central Park features leisure, sport, family, and tourist activities, as well as a Climatorium, or visitor center, shown here.
2 Artificial cooling devices emit mist or rain to lower the surrounding air temperature.
3 The Gradient Darkness Pavillon, made of wood, is one of twelve solar-powered pavilions that punctuate the park.

Paris-based architect Philippe Rahm is one of very few individuals in the field of architecture whose practice is focused on not figuratively but literally designing atmospheres. For Rahm, form follows climate. In a project to design both landscape and architecture of Central Park — a new public space on the site of a former airport on the generally hot, humid subtropical island of Taiwan — Rahm and his team gave themselves the task to create an optimal design for each microclimate. His firm began by evaluating the site and producing three vast ground maps, showing heat, humidity, and pollution conditions, and concluded with a microclimate map, which identified four "coolia" (cool areas), three "dryia" (dry areas), and four "clearia" (clean air areas), assigning them various activities according to climatic suitability. The completed park, a continuous, 1.2-mi.-long (2 km) landscape, includes twelve solar-powered pavilions, each dedicated to one of the twelve senses identified by philosopher Rudolf Steiner: touch, life, movement, balance, smell, taste, sight, warmth, hearing, landscape, concept, and ego. Sensors are placed every 164 ft. (50 m) to measure air temperature, sunshine, wind, humidity, and air-pollution levels in real time. This data is used to generate a map of the park that is accessible on smartphones, revealing a usually invisible landscape of climatic conditions and allowing visitors to adapt their route according to the needs of all their senses.

Visionaries

Central Park, Philippe Rahm architectes
Taichung, Taiwan, 2020

4
5

38

4 A climatic map of Central Park showing how different zones vary in terms of heat, humidity, and pollution.
5 The maps show the artificial cooling systems utilized throughout the park.
6 Interior view of the Dryium, which maintains the temperature, humidity, and light conditions of November 21 — a day recognized in Taichung for having the best possible climatic conditions of the year.
7 The maintenance center is one of a dozen pavilions installed in the park.

Visionaries

In the Robot Skies, Liam Young
2016

1

1   *In the Robot Skies* was shot entirely with autonomous drones.
2   The rooftop of a council-estate tower block in London, above which a network of surveillance drones monitors residents.
3   In the film's sci-fi scenario, a teenager looks to hijack a surveillance drone as it cruises overhead.

Liam Young is a visionary Australian designer, critic, curator, educator, and filmmaker based in Los Angeles, California. As part of the Unknown Fields studio, he travels on annual expeditions to extraordinary landscapes, from Chernobyl to the Far North region of Alaska and Madagascar. His practice imagines alternative worlds as a means to understand our own in original ways, co-opting narratives of radical storytelling. His production *In the Robot Skies* is the first narrative short film shot entirely with drones, and is based on a story written by science-fiction author Tim Maughan. The film uses the drone not just as an instrument of visual storytelling but also demonstrates its use as a tool for antisurveillance activists in the future. From the eyes of the drones, the film depicts two teenagers each held by police order within the digital confines of his or her own council-estate tower block in London. A network of drones surveys the council estates, forcing the two characters to stay apart. They pass notes to each other via their own hacked and decorated drones, like kids in an old-fashioned classroom, scribbling messages on paper, balling them up, and stowing them in their aircraft. In this near-future city, drones not only serve as agents of state surveillance, but also become the aerial vehicles through which the two teens fall in love.

Visionaries

Color(ed) Theory, Amanda Williams
Chicago, IL, USA, 2014–16

Referencing the research-oriented experimental practice of painter Josef Albers and the detailed color theories of Le Corbusier, Amanda Williams — a visual artist, architect, and academic — set out to search for a palette that responds to the spatial and social politics of color in the urban landscape where she grew up, in a neighborhood in South Chicago. Her ongoing series *Color(ed) Theory* explores how objective and subjective definitions of color exist in veiled language used in American media and popular culture to describe racially charged city spaces. Her work explores questions such as: What color is urban? What color is gentrification? What color is privilege? What color is poverty? She started by taking cultural references from ubiquitous products whose names would first vividly conjure a color: the neon turquoise of hair product Ultra Sheen, the searing orange of a bag of Flamin' Hot Cheetos, or the deep purple of a Crown Royal bag. Once the palette was established, she reflected on government-led disinvestment and segregation of Black communities. In painting her culturally coded palette onto the facades of abandoned houses, marked for demolition, Williams poignantly uses color to stress this history of her city: in communities where the drivers for development have acted against the interests of residents for decades, it is in the destruction of their environment where the agency of architecture is most familiar, not in its rebuilding.

1

1 *Color(ed) Theory: Currency Exchange/Safe Passage*, 2014–16.
2 *Color(ed) Theory: Flamin' Red Hots*, 2014–16.
3 *Color(ed) Theory: Crown Royal Bag*, 2014–16.
4 *Color(ed) Theory: Ultrasheen*, 2014–16.

2

3

4

43

DMZ Vault of Life and Knowledge, Mass Studies
2015

On the border between North and South Korea, a strip of no-man's-land called the "demilitarized zone" (DMZ) has been the subject of ever more cultural and political discourse. The zone has been completely abandoned since 1952, but in recent years the possibility for a thawing of relations between north and south has seemed stronger, and artists and architects have reimagined what the role of this land could be. Many of the fantasies about the future of the DMZ are propelled by its extraordinary condition as an ecologically diverse environment, home to almost two thousand different organisms, including more than one hundred endangered species. In 2015, artist Jae-Eun Choi commissioned a series of fictional projects that envision a new life for the landscape of the DMZ. The speculative design for the Vault of Life and Knowledge is by Seoul–based architect Minsuk Cho, who is the founder of Mass Studies, a studio committed to the discourse of architecture through practice and research, from major building projects to scholarly exhibitions. Cho's design for a future seed bank and ecology library is an adaptive reuse of one of four existing incursion tunnels. This proposal would enable both North and South Korea to contribute to a shared purpose: to study, protect, and nurture the ecology of the DMZ as a symbol of hope.

4

1   Section of Minsuk Cho's speculative design for the Vault of Life and Knowledge, a future seed bank and ecology library in the DMZ.
2   An image showing the construction of the vault underway.
3   A monolithic podium as part of the Vault of Life site in the north.
4   Here, looking from the south to the north, is the "Center," where the tunnel crosses the Military Demarcation Line. This is the starting point of the two vaults. The Vault of Life will extend northward, while the Vault of Knowledge will grow toward the south, forming one continuous structure within the existing tunnel.

Visionaries

Opalis, Rotor DC
Brussels, Belgium, 2012–

Belgian design practice Rotor has expanded to being two-pronged since it was established in 2005. On one side, its team works on traditional architecture and interior design commissions, as well as producing exhibitions, books, and research. On the other, Rotor DC is a self-contained company dedicated to architectural salvage, a form of material rescue for the hugely wasteful renovation and demolition process that takes place all over the world. Rotor DC assists in the salvation and reuse of existing materials, such as ceramic tiles, window frames, wooden floors, concrete panels, steel pipes, and metal studs. The team works with other architects, building owners, and contractors to dismantle, condition, and sell materials to avoid them being scrapped. Given that the manufacture of concrete alone generates around 8 percent of global carbon dioxide emissions, companies in the architecture and construction industries such as Rotor DC are making a shift toward sustainability by reusing a greater proportion of construction materials. In 2012, Rotor DC created an online directory of retailers across Europe and the UK trading in salvaged materials. This directory, which is called Opalis, helps designers, architects, contractors, and building owners reuse materials that previously would have been discarded in landfills.

1

1 Roof tiles that have been dismantled from their original site now stored in the yard at Deeterink Dakpannenhandel in Buurse, Netherlands, near the German border.
2 An assortment of recycled wood beams — at Sloopwerken Van Kessel & Zn in Sint-Oedenrode, Netherlands — available to be used in a new project.
3 Stacks of sorted and cleaned bricks at Walstra Antieke Bouwmaterialen in Bolsward, Netherlands.
4 Valuable elements, such as steel pipes, are sourced from buildings slated for demolition and offered for resale at Cleveland Steel & Tubes in Thirsk, England, UK.

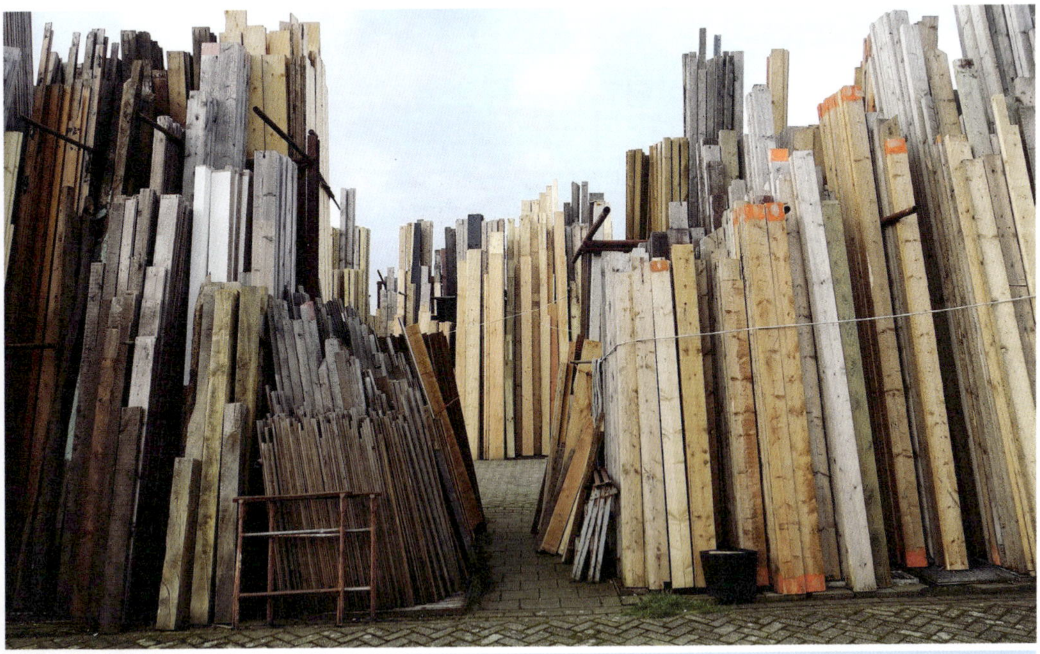
2

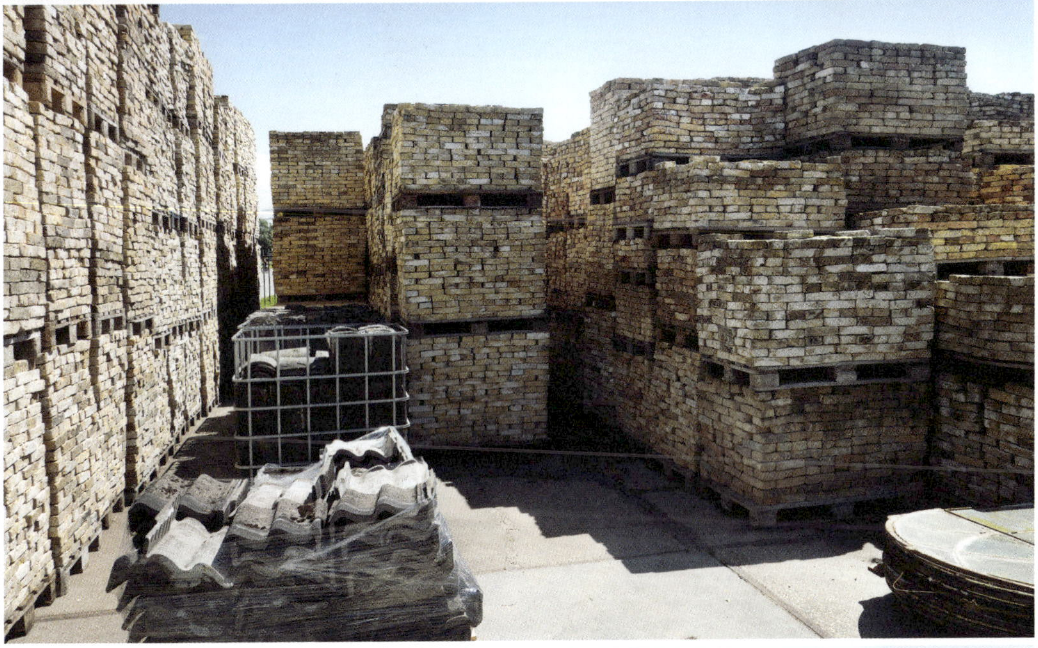
3

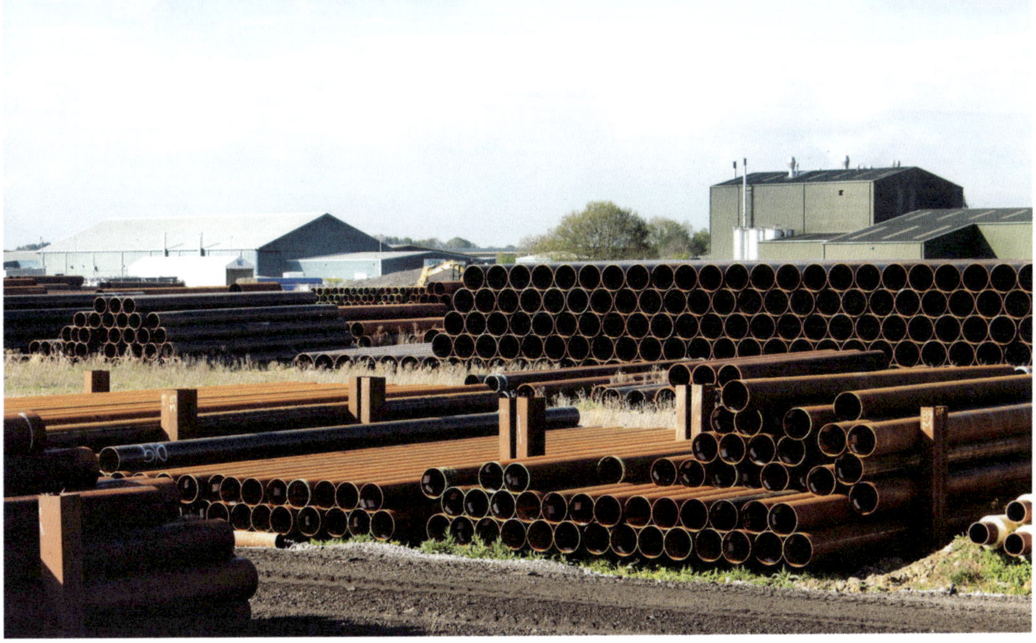
4

Marching On, Bryony Roberts, Mabel O. Wilson, and the Marching Cobras of New York
New York, NY, USA, 2017

Designers and researchers Bryony Roberts and Mabel O. Wilson collaborated with the Marching Cobras, an after-school drumline and dance team based in the Harlem neighborhood of New York City, to create this performance and exhibition project. Commissioned by the non-profit organization Storefront for Art and Architecture, the work included an exhibition sharing the historical context of this powerful and traditional form of cultural expression in the African American community, as well as a public performance as part of the Performa 17 biennial program. The phenomenon of drill teams — groups of usually young people in military costume who march and dance to drums, cymbals, and other percussion in public — takes on a new tenor in a time when increasing surveillance of open space and the militarization of police has politicized New York's parks and sidewalks. Roberts and Wilson here celebrated the long tradition of marching band and drill team as a way for young people to present themselves and occupy public space with creativity, to test their bodies, and to express themselves as youths with confidence. The costumes for the performance were designed with double-sided camouflage so the performers could blend into and then pop out of the landscape.

1 Historically rooted in military training exercises and combat formations, African American marching bands and drumlines honored service in US conflicts and highlighted the absence of civil rights despite sacrifices to defend the nation.
2 In part, marching bands served as a form of camouflage that enabled African Americans to gather and occupy public spaces when this was otherwise prohibited during the era of Jim Crow segregation.
3 The fabrics used for the costumes merged military camouflage with the geometric paving patterns of Marcus Garvey Park in the Harlem neighborhood of New York City, site of the *Marching On* performances.

Visionaries

Marching On, Bryony Roberts, Mabel O. Wilson, and the Marching Cobras of New York
New York, NY, USA, 2017

4 Members of the Marching Cobras of New York mid-performance.
5 Artwork created for the accompanying exhibition, depicting the Marching Cobras in geometric pixelation.
6 While their choreography has radically expanded since the nineteenth century to incorporate other forms of movement, including dance lines, hip-hop, and step choreography, marching bands still remain connected to a lineage of marching as political expression.
7 A Marching Cobra drummer rendered mid-movement. The artwork shows off the hybrid patterns created for the costumes and custom-printed fabrics used throughout the exhibition design.

Visionaries

CLIMAVORE: On Tidal Zones, Cooking Sections
Isle of Skye, Scotland, UK, 2015–

Cooking Sections — a London–based duo operating between installation, research, and activism — investigates and responds to the new landscapes and unexpected phenomena created by climate change, often using food as a way to understand those changes. On Tidal Zones is an installation on the Isle of Skye in Scotland that uses a temporary dining experience to highlight the environmental effects of the island's specific aquaculture. The local economy is dependent on industrial salmon farming, but decades of heavy antibiotics and pink dyes used by farmers have contaminated the water in the region, threatening the survival of the sea and landscape. Cooking Sections established a series of interventions, such as educational workshops, apprenticeships, and guidance for anyone to set up an oyster or seaweed farm. Each day at low tide, a series of "oyster tables" emerges above the sea and operates as a public dining table for performative meals. The team works with chefs of local restaurants to create dishes utilizing species that nurture the marine ecology: seaweed, oysters, clams, and mussels. On Tidal Zones is part of a wider series of interventions, called CLIMAVORE, which raises awareness of the environmental impacts of intensive food infrastructures, promoting instead a diet that is based on mainly regenerative ingredients in response to the climate emergency.

1 The project is situated in an intertidal zone at Bayfield in Portree, Isle of Skye, Scotland. At high tide the installation functions as an underwater multispecies oyster bed.
2 Every day at low tide, the installation emerges above the sea.
3 Aerial view of the project functioning as a dining table for humans.

Visionaries

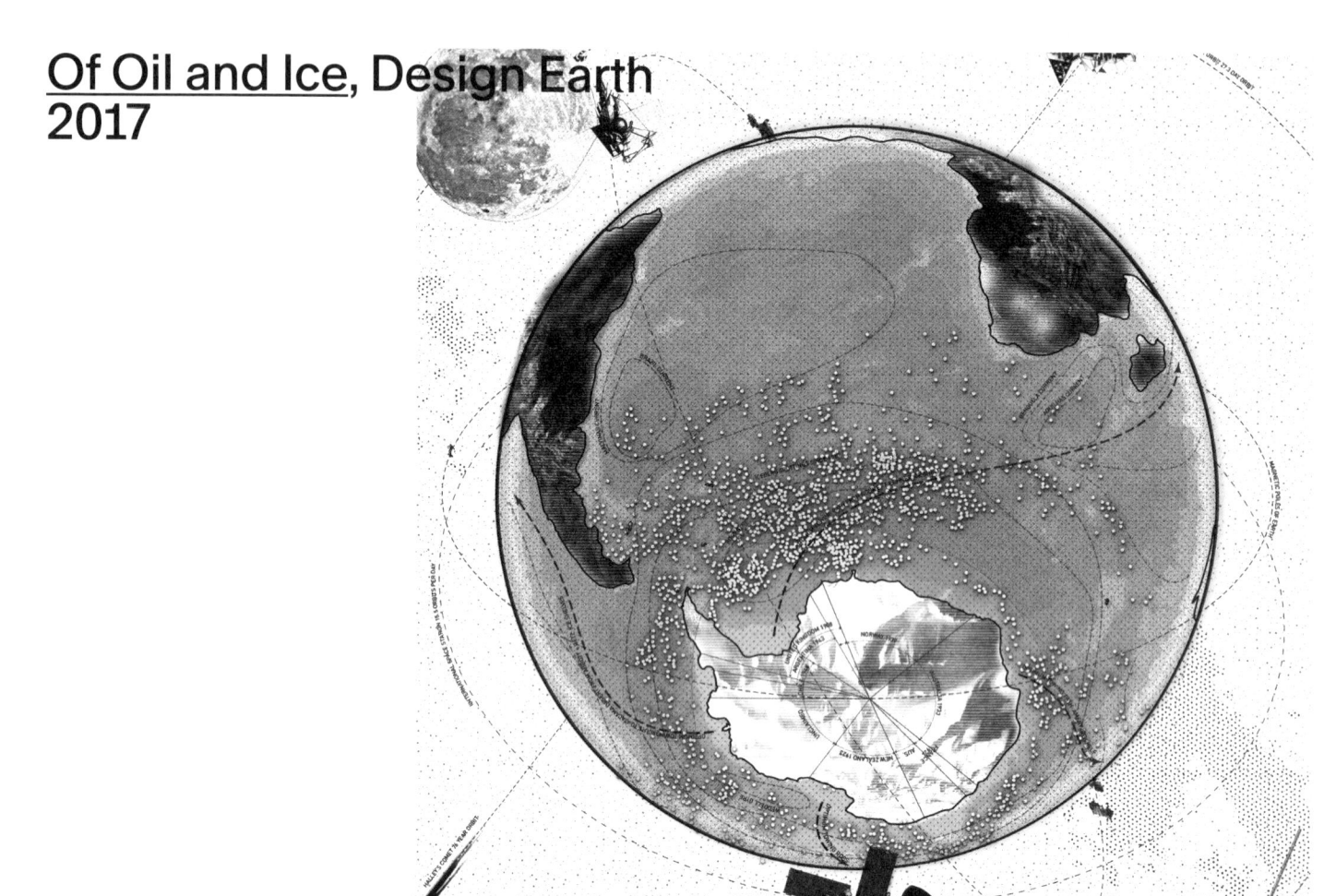

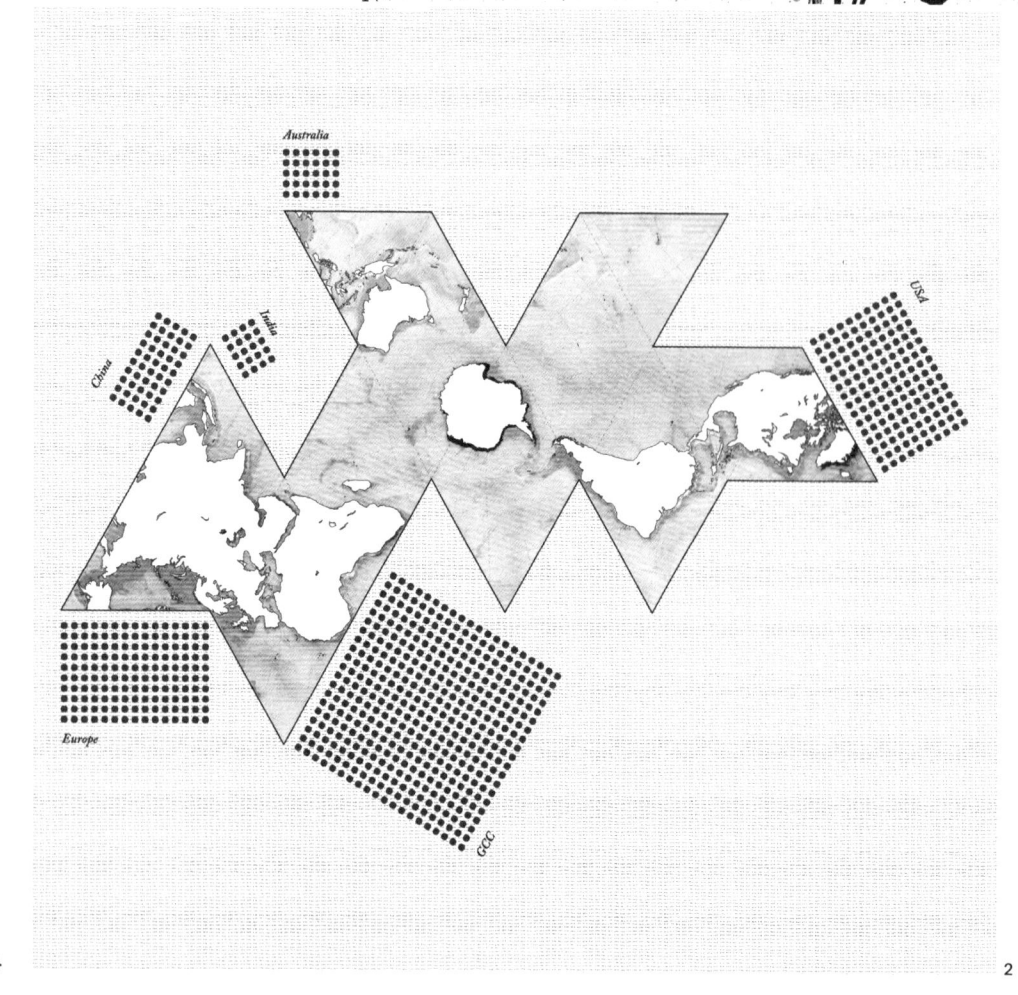

Of Oil and Ice, Design Earth
2017

Addressing the planetary-scale environmental crisis, Design Earth — comprising academics and architects El Hadi Jazairy and Rania Ghosn — argues that there is a paralysis of representation in the discussion of climate change; for decades the statistics, charts, and aerial photography used to convey the habitat loss and rising temperatures of our planet have remained consistent. *Of Oil and Ice* is a sequence of large-scale drawings that adopts the nineteenth-century tradition of beautifully etched diorama illustrations to imagine a world that marries the melting icebergs in Antarctica and the impending droughts and water shortages facing the arid but oil-rich societies in the Gulf. After running a series of workshops on the notion of "iceberg utilization," the story fantastically proposes that the icecaps, which represent 326 quadrillion gallons of fresh water, journey for one hundred days to the perimeter of the Hormuz Dam in the Gulf, where they would be sliced and then stored in custom-made towers. There the ice would melt, becoming part of a freshwater aqueduct that could replace the energy-intensive desalinization factories that populate the region. The icebergs could supply water for commercial and domestic use, reducing the oil used to fuel existing water desalination systems. This ecological fiction invites its audience to engage with the scales of the earth.

3

1 Antarctica calves 95 percent of the world's iceberg mass, or an estimated 326 quadrillion gallons of fresh water.
2 The Dymaxion map positions Antarctica at the center of a thirsty world. Antarctica, which holds 75 percent of Earth's fresh water, is represented in relation to the global capacity for desalination.
3 An iceberg is towed by three ships toward the Gulf, flanked by helicopters.

Of Oil and Ice, Design Earth
2017

56

4   After one hundred days at sea, the icebergs approach the Hormuz Dam. This megaproject is part of the future "Critical Water Security Plan," which protects the Gulf region's shores from rising sea levels. Generating hydropower, it channels the iceberg's cooling effects to sustain agriculture in coastal humid microclimates.
5   Antarctica has the largest and oldest ice mass on the planet. Like an icy archive of natural history, it holds the world's best data on the global carbon cycle and Earth's climatic history.
6   The ice has to melt in controlled water towers, some of which are designed as miniatures of iconic regional structures, such as the Burj Khalifa in Dubai, United Arab Emirates, and the Great Mosque of Samarra in Iraq.
7   The berg as it passes from the ice dome into the Strait of Hormuz Dam. Here, it begins to make its transition to fresh water.

insiders

Many clients still subscribe to the idea that an iconic building by a famous architect will be a generator of economic success and positive publicity. But just as the dubious portmanteau of starchitect is, thankfully, fading into obscurity, more progressive businesses and institutions are now skeptical of design by name alone. Today's most acclaimed architects — those receiving high-profile projects on an international stage — ensure that the built work they produce responds sensitively to its site, addresses the climate crisis, and promotes positive societal change, which is seen as an intrinsic part of excellent design. Whether by deeply investing in their communities, working in unexpected media, or collaborating outside their discipline, many of the world's most innovative studios are subverting, expanding, and challenging the briefs set by their clients and taking the opportunity to transform regular design projects into Trojan horses for meaningful change from inside the industry. The architects and designers included here are first asking themselves if they really must build at all, and then, if they must, the questions continue: How can this project contribute to the social fabric of its neighborhood? What more can a roof, a wall, a park be and do? How can the physical manifestation of a new institution or museum, for example, honor its immaterial goals through the very process of the building's realization? How can they understand and intervene in the supply chain involved in both materials and labor used in the project? The practitioners within this chapter know how to be instigators, fundraisers, collaborators, and planners, and tactically use their profile to raise the bar for others. It is exciting to know that a signature style of the next generation of high-profile architects is not a formal or material fad, but a visionary approach to ethical responsibility.

Zeitz MOCCA, Heatherwick Studio
Cape Town, South Africa, 2017

1

1   Entrance to Zeitz MOCCA. On the left, the original dust tower of the grain silo, which functioned as a giant vacuum cleaner in the silo's heyday, has been retained and will eventually play host to site-specific installations.
2   Faceted windows installed on the upper levels of the building have a lantern-like appearance.

An array of geodesic glass windows protrudes from the concrete frame of one of Cape Town's most recognizable industrial buildings, signaling to passersby, and indeed anyone who encounters an image of the building, its spectacular transformation from a former grain silo — disused since the 1990s — into the world's largest museum of contemporary art from Africa and its diaspora. In order to make a new space for the museum, Heatherwick Studio scooped away the center of forty-two separate cellular silo tubes. This gesture generated a spectacular atrium and follows artist Gordon Matta-Clark's approach of "making space without building it." This design was mapped out with complex modeling techniques, then painstakingly realized by reinforcing each of the hollow structures before cutting them with double-blade handsaws. Each of the cut edges was then polished to a smooth finish. The result is a dramatic perspective of the museum's new inner sanctum, a vaulted contemporary cathedral that gives visitors an X-ray view into the building's history. The new museum holds eighty gallery spaces, a sculpture garden, and a hotel, and underground tunnels have also been adapted for artists to create site-specific works. Thomas Heatherwick felt it was important to reconnect with the building's preexisting materiality and stripped off many layers of white paint to reveal the original concrete, which was made with dirt from nearby Table Mountain.

Insiders

Zeitz MOCCA, Heatherwick Studio
Cape Town, South Africa, 2017

3   A facade of the existing elevator tower now forms part of the new atrium. Its original coating of paint was water jetted off to reveal the textured concrete.
4   The full-height atrium is an organically shaped void carved out of the concrete tubes that once stored grain.
5   The top six floors of the fifteen-story building were converted into a hotel.
6   Visitors taking photographs of the huge atrium.

Insiders

NAVE, Smiljan Radić
Santiago, Chile, 2016

A secondhand circus tent sits at the top of NAVE, an experimental performing arts center in Santiago. In 2010 an earthquake and several subsequent fires nearly destroyed the houses on this block, which is in a run-down area of the Chilean capital; only the neoclassical facade, itself a replica from the 1940s, of the existing building remained partially intact. Chilean architect Smiljan Radić used a very dark grey in-situ cast concrete to construct all the interior spaces; soft, bright felt and hanging structures serve as temporary, flexible space dividers for performance spaces, rehearsal rooms, and offices. The roof of the building was identified by the architect as a natural area for an outdoor pavilion, but the government wouldn't give planning permission for something modern that would disrupt the remaining neoclassical facade. Radić's solution was to purchase a family circus tent, arguing that it is temporary, light, easy to manipulate, and beautiful. The circus tent is an elemental way to watch performances, and it is also symbolic — expressive of affordable and low-tech design, which was necessary to the project being completed within budget. In stark contrast to the dark, cavelike design of the interior spaces, the NAVE's pinnacle is a bright, ephemeral readymade, its temporary playfulness, vivid colors, and childlike forms paying homage to radical architects of the past: Cedric Price and Aldo Rossi.

1   NAVE occupies the corner of a city block in the Yungay neighborhood of Santiago.
2   A concrete floor on the rooftop is painted bright red to match the underside of a secondhand circus tent acquired by the architect to function as an outdoor performance space for the center.
3   The performance spaces feature bright white interiors.
4   By contrast, other areas of the center feature dark-colored walls and floors.

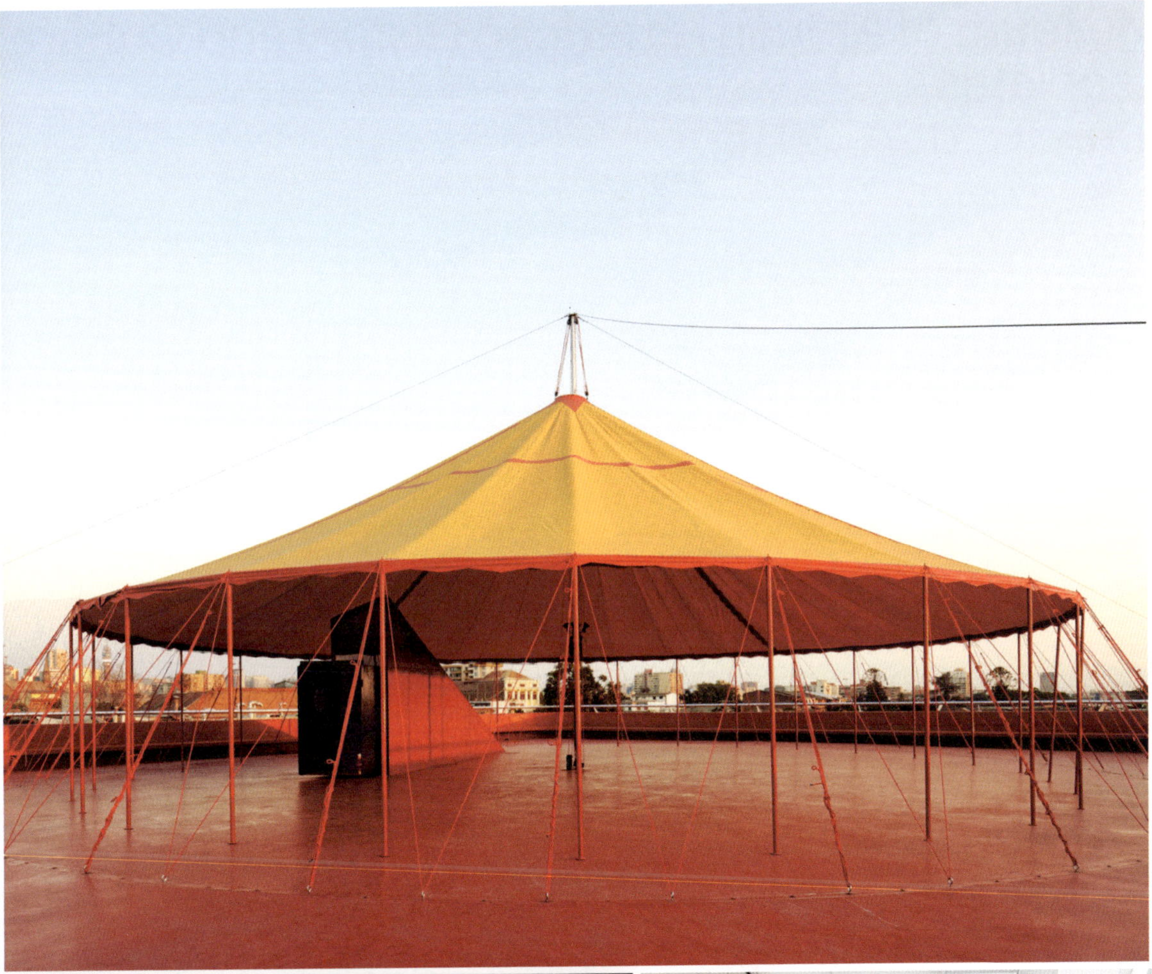

2

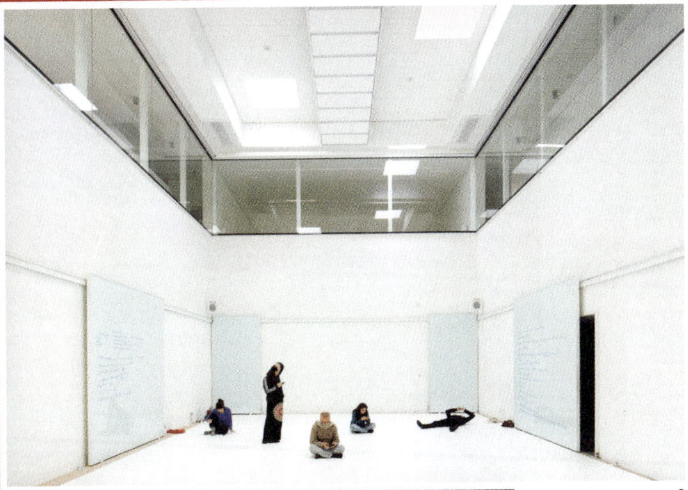

3

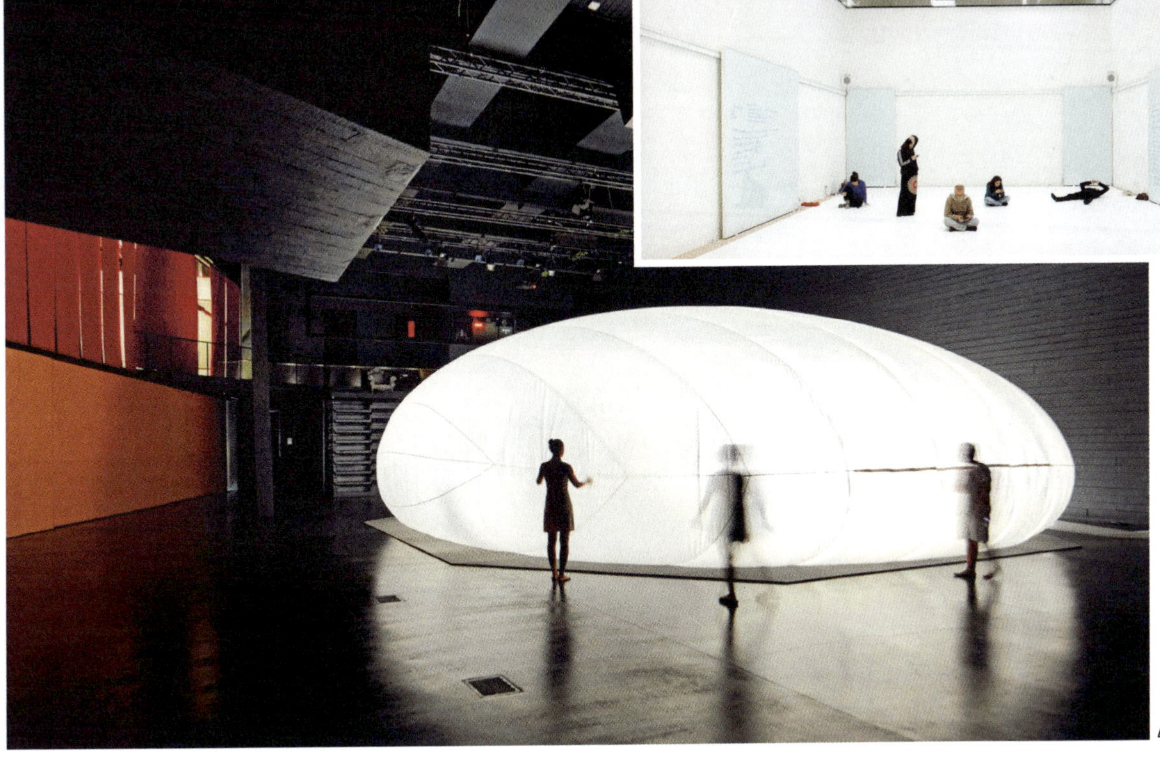

4

National Museum of African American History and Culture,
Adjaye Associates
Washington, DC, USA, 2016

1   Exterior view of the National Museum of African American History and Culture, which comprises three stacked volumes.

National Museum of African American History and Culture, Adjaye Associates
Washington, DC, USA, 2016

Dedicated to the history of African American culture, this museum of the Smithsonian Institution was completed in 2016 by London–, New York–, and Accra, Ghana–based firm Adjaye Associates. Designed in the form of a three-tiered crown motif from the West African country Benin, it is both a celebration of African American culture and a recognition of that community's deeply traumatic history. In taking on this monumental task, the office's principal architect Sir David Adjaye sought to explore what a twenty-first-century museum should be. Dismantling traditional assumptions of display and deification of objects, the Ghanaian–British architect and his team designed a narrative-led space amalgamating architecture with history and memory. Every element of the building, from its bones to its skin, tells a story. The building facade is a cloak of dark, shimmering sand-cast bronze, both the material and its pattern chosen by Adjaye as a homage to the craftsmanship of West African slaves whose delicate metalwork details have ornamented houses in Charleston, South Carolina, and New Orleans. The building is situated on the National Mall in Washington, DC. Adjaye Associates located the main circulation pathways along the museum's perimeter, where a series of strategically placed windows afford views of some of the most portentous structures in the United States, including the White House, US Capitol, Washington Monument, and Martin Luther King, Jr. Memorial.

2   Patterns in the bronze filigree screens derive from the decorative metalwork created by African American craftsmen in cities such as New Orleans and Charleston, South Carolina.
3   The ornamental bronze exterior lattice creates transparency and allows sunlight into the interior atrium.

Insiders 69

Ocho Quebradas House, Elemental
Los Vilos, Chile, 2013

Founder of Chilean architecture studio Elemental, Alejandro Aravena received the Pritzker Prize in 2016 in part for his revolutionary approach to social housing that allowed residents in the city of Iquique to finance and complete their own homes in stages — the idea being that they were provided "half a good house,"[2] which the residents could then complete with their own labor. Aravena and team showed a different aspect of their practice with Ocho Quebradas House, a residence designed for a beautiful but extreme environment. This weekend retreat is part of a development designed by eight firms each from across Chile and Japan that were invited to imagine original ways of inhabiting this striking and wild terrain fronting the Pacific Ocean.

Viewing a second residence as not being strictly necessary, Elemental took the opportunity to question domestic conventions. The main living space is conceived as a low slab, which opens up to the sky through a tilted second volume that serves as a chimney. The vertical third mass contains a stack of bedrooms with panoramic views of the sea. In response to the rugged geography of the site and strong winds, the project was designed to feel like architecture at its most essential, and it uses only three materials: wood, glass, and reinforced concrete. The ventilation and heating systems are simple too; natural cross ventilation cools the spaces, and a gas-fired boiler and hot-water radiators provide heat.

1 From the exterior, the vacation home appears to be three singular monoliths, but these interconnected and cantilevered volumes form one spectacular house.
2 With shutters closed, the upper volume has a highly sculptural appearance. The main living space opens toward the elements.

Ocho Quebradas House, Elemental
Los Vilos, Chile, 2013

3 Traces of the wooden formwork can be seen in the surface of the poured concrete.
4 Instead of a chimney the house has a firepit, which the architects chose to include because it is one of the most revolutionary yet oldest achievements of humankind.
5 The house is intended to be enjoyed for its primitive design. Inhabitants can allow themselves to go back to a more simple way of life.
6 Above the firepit an oversize oblong aperture lets in light and acts as a chute for smoke.

Insiders

Lycée Schorge, Kéré Architecture
Gando, Burkina Faso, 2015

Architect Francis Kéré is lauded for his institutional, cultural, and educational initiatives, and experimental and elegant use of naturally occurring, affordable materials. He brings this special form of contemporary architecture to the village of Gando, where he grew up, which is in the landlocked country of Burkina Faso in western Africa. One of the poorest regions in the continent, it has a literacy rate of just 20 percent and there is little access to electricity and water. In 2001, after completing his architectural training in Germany, Kéré orchestrated the funding and building of a primary school for his village; the project, throughout its construction, provided work, training, and social space, demonstrating that architecture can expand beyond its primary function. In Lycée Schorge, a secondary school, Kéré wanted to address the issue of ventilation and humidity in an environment where temperatures can rise up to 104 degrees Fahrenheit (40 degrees Celsius) in the shade, and there is no air-conditioning. He built the school in a radial form around a central courtyard, with an undulating overhanging roof for air circulation, and wind-catching towers that cool the interior and expel hot stagnant air. Kéré wrapped the whole building in a tall, elegant screen of eucalyptus wood. Usually used for scaffolding, the tree trunks create an additional sheltered space as an alternative to being in the classroom, as well as protection from dust and wind.

1 A sheltered exterior space immediately surrounds the classrooms.
2 Louvers encourage ventilation and the wavelike pattern of plaster on the ceiling allows hot stagnant air to be expelled.
3 The screen made of eucalyptus wood with the wind-catching towers visible at top.

Lycée Schorge, Kéré Architecture
Gando, Burkina Faso, 2015

4

4   The wind towers are visible from the air, as is an orchard of young trees planted to the south of the school.
5   Small buckets of water can be placed underneath the benches to provide humidity for the hot, dry classrooms.
6   Eucalyptus-wood benches are tucked into the facade of the building, offering shaded spots to sit.
7   The role of the school is intended to go beyond the teaching of schoolchildren and to provide a community space that invests in education and training for everyone in the village.

5

Insiders 77

Fuyang Cultural Complex, Amateur Architecture Studio
Fuyang, China, 2017

1

1 Aerial view of the Fuyang Cultural Complex and surrounding region.
2 The wavelike roof design references ancient Chinese calligraphy and painting, and is navigable via staircases and paths.
3 The complex is clad in recycled tiles.

The practice of Amateur Architecture Studio is rooted in the culture and natural resources of the communities in which the firm works. After receiving an invitation from a regional government to design a landmark new cultural complex in the small town of Fuyang, near the city of Hangzhou, the studio responded with a conditional answer. It would design the complex only if the same administration agreed to organize and fund the preservation and restoration of the nearby rural village of Wencun. Like many remote Chinese villages, Wencun had experienced an exodus of young people to the cities, and the remaining housing and infrastructure were in poor repair. Amateur Architecture Studio's objective was to encourage a new generation to settle in the village and to integrate ancient building methods and materials typical of the region into its rehabilitation. For the design of the Fuyang Cultural Complex, the studio used construction materials that were common in the village, such as rammed earth and crushed rubble, giving the center a tactile quality and creating a powerful sense of contextuality. The form of the complex was inspired by the landscape paintings of a fourteenth-century Yuan dynasty artist whose depictions of the picturesque mountains behind are mirrored in the design of the sweeping rooflines.

Insiders

Polis Station, Studio Gang
Chicago, IL, USA, 2015

Demand for radical police reform within the United States reached a zenith in the spring of 2020 following the killing of George Floyd in Minneapolis which ignited a movement of millions to protest against police brutality, mass incarceration, and systemic racial injustices. The city of Minneapolis promised to dismantle its police department, and other cities have vowed major structural reform. While many of these ideas for reform require top-level macro issues to be federally mandated, American architect Jeanne Gang — partner and founder of Studio Gang — has demonstrated how they can touch down at the hyperlocal level. Her 2015 proposal explores how the physical site of police stations can be a space for change. Asking if stations could be redesigned to holistically promote public safety and better relationships between police officers and the communities they serve, Studio Gang held discussions with residents, community leaders, and police in Chicago to ask how police stations — with their own complex semiotics and architectural history — could become neighborhood assets offering desired amenities and services. As part of their resulting proposal for the 10th District station, Gang's team built a basketball court on an unused portion of the parking lot where local youths and police can let off steam and shoot hoops, creating an environment for grassroots dialogue.

1. Through talking and sketching with local students, Studio Gang learned about the spaces and programs they wanted to see in their neighborhood.
2. This proposal demonstrates how police stations can become full-service community centers that improve public safety, enhance social cohesion, and strengthen the economy of the surrounding neighborhood.
3. At "Community Cafe" workshops, Studio Gang led conversations with residents of Chicago's 10th District to learn how their police station could offer more activities and amenities.

Insiders

Palestinian Museum, Heneghan Peng
Birzeit, Palestine, 2017

1. The limestone-clad building is fronted by a series of zigzagging gardens.
2. Aerial view of the Palestinian Museum. The building emerges from the landscape to create a strong profile for the hilltop.

High up in the Palestine hills, north of the West Bank city Ramallah, the Palestinian Museum looks toward the Mediterranean Sea. This cultural hub for the Taawon (Welfare Association) — a humanitarian group working to support Palestinian communities in the West Bank and Gaza Strip, as well as refugee camps in Lebanon — was conceived as a way to share the complex stories and multidimensional identities of Palestinian communities and cultures through exhibitions, public programs, and workshops. Irish architecture firm Heneghan Peng's design features bright limestone walls, window shades in the form of jet-black fins, and angular contours zigzagging the building's footprint in plan. The work draws on the history of the site's once-agricultural land, as well as its topography, building upon the ruins of early fieldstone walls used by local farmers. Each newly designed terrace has a different identity: closest to the building are cultured and domesticated terraces of citrus trees and aromatic herbs; as the terraces descend to the west, the planting features indigenous species. Publicly accessible platforms are integrated into scenic paths, providing zones for performances, markets, and art classes. The project has transformed what was once a productive landscape for food — depleted by the systematic seizure of farmland in Palestine since Israeli occupation — into a productive landscape for art and culture too.

Palestinian Museum, Heneghan Peng
Birzeit, Palestine, 2017

3 Stone found on site was used to build retaining walls supporting a series of cascading terraces.
4 A group of students on a visit to the museum.
5 Rows of black fins on the building exterior provide some shade.
6 View of the ground floor, which includes the entrance reception and stairs leading to the Education and Research Center.

Art Biotop Water Garden, Junya Ishigami + Associates
Nasu, Japan, 2018

1   As well as transposing more than 300 trees to the site, Ishigami constructed 160 artificial ponds surrounded by moss, creating miniature habitats for the local plant species, insects, and wildlife.

Art Biotop Water Garden, Junya Ishigami + Associates
Nasu, Japan, 2018

Japanese architect Junya Ishigami is known for his keen sensitivity to the relationship between the natural world and the built environment. The idea for the dreamlike Art Biotop Water Garden was born when it became apparent the construction of a hotel in the idyllic mountain town of Nasu, Japan, would mean the felling of a large section of a forest. In response to this situation, Ishigami proposed instead to preserve the trees and replant all 318 within an adjacent meadow. Over the course of four years, each and every tree was meticulously measured, uprooted, and transported, the process resulting in a garden that incorporates 160 artificial ponds surrounded by moss, wildflowers, pathways, and a series of miniature habitats for insects, local plant species, and wildlife. A subterranean network of pipes connected to a nearby river irrigates the labyrinthine garden. The resulting environment is of a higher density of ponds and trees than could ever be found in a "natural" ecosystem, and yet Ishigami proposes that this clearly artificial landscape is no more or less natural than what was there before. Part of his reasoning for embedding existing trees into their new site was that in recent history the location had been both a rice field and, later, a man-made meadow — with this project Ishigami transposes a forest and superimposes formerly separate layers of history in a single space.

2 The mazelike landscape is navigated via delicate stone pathways.
3 A subterranean network of pipes connected to a nearby river ensures that water flows throughout the site year-round and that water levels are controlled.
4 This drawing demonstrates the removal of trees from one site to go to another.

meadow

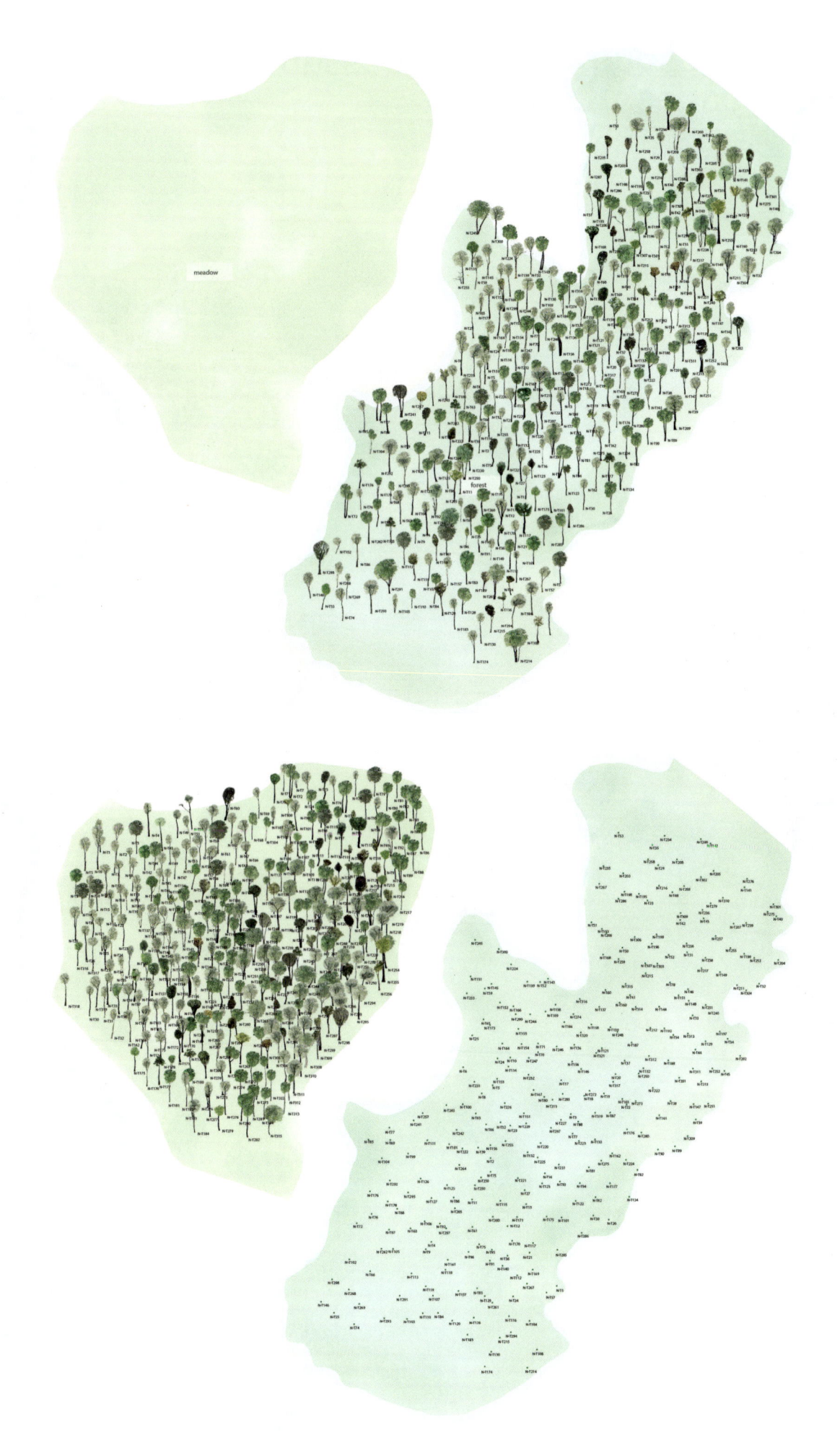

forest

Bait Ur Rouf Mosque, Marina Tabassum
Dhaka, Bangladesh, 2012

Bangladesh is a country crisscrossed by water. The interconnectivity between rivers and earth is one of the enduring themes of life in its capital, Dhaka. Local architect Marina Tabassum's built practice is guided by the relationship of land and flows of goods and peoples, with all of her work striving to connect with and contribute to the legacy of Bengal. One of her most revered works began when Tabassum's grandmother ceded part of her land, in a densely populated area of Dhaka, to the city, and asked Tabassum to help her build a mosque there. Throughout the four-year construction phase, she acted simultaneously as the architect, client, builder, and fundraiser. To accommodate a low budget, the design used the barest of materials, predominantly perforated baked earth bricks. Built on a stepped plinth that acts as an approachable public space, the mosque is deliberately accessed off axis and bears no symbolic connection with most mosques of recent history; its corners are open, allowing shafts of daylight to move through the building's prayer spaces like a sundial. Within the complexity of Bangladesh, where rapidly and poorly constructed commercial developments are the go-to form of urbanism, Tabassum here refers to architecture that is tightly tied to the nature of its environment as a form of "architectural resistance."

1 Neighborhood children playing outside the terra-cotta brick mosque.
2 Perforations in the exterior wall allow star-like patterns of diffused light to enter the building, as well as providing natural ventilation.

Bait Ur Rouf Mosque, Marina Tabassum
Dhaka, Bangladesh, 2012

4

3 The architecture plays with intersections of geometric volumes to create symbolic movement of light and shadow throughout the mosque.
4 The building sits comfortably in its context, providing a community space at the heart of its neighborhood.
5 Interior view of the prayer hall, with hanging fans and dappled light from small ceiling apertures.

5

93

CopenHill, BIG
Copenhagen, Denmark, 2019

Bjarke Ingels, founding partner and creative director of Copenhagen–, New York–, London–, and Barcelona–based firm BIG, describes his vision for the future of architecture as "hedonistic sustainability" — he believes that working in conscientious ways that mitigate climate change and designing exciting buildings should not be mutually exclusive. CopenHill, a large hybrid power plant and ski slope, is his firm's scheme for a clean-energy power plant. The studio fused the facility with an idea to build a mountain for the city's many fervent skiers, who, due to Denmark's flat topography, had to travel to neighboring Sweden to access the slopes. The meadow that stretches from the top of the aluminum-clad industrial building to its bottom includes a café, a 328-ft.-high (100 m) climbing wall, a forest area, and a number of hiking trails. The incinerator is engineered to generate clean energy from 485,000 tons (440,000 tonnes) of household waste, providing electricity and heating for over 150,000 homes per year. CopenHill is the closest the studio has come to its goal of realizing buildings designed to be man-made ecosystems that intelligently respond to environmental challenges. The studio is also working on other projects of ambitious global scale, including an urban master plan for Japanese car manufacturer Toyota with wooden buildings and self-driving vehicles and the BIG U, a proposed protective system from future storm surges extending 10 mi. (16 km) around Lower Manhattan as part of the work of the Hurricane Sandy Rebuilding Task Force.

1 Exterior of CopenHill, also known as the Amager Resource Center, wrapped by a checkerboard grid facade.
2 Aerial view of CopenHill showing the ski slope in vibrant greens.

2

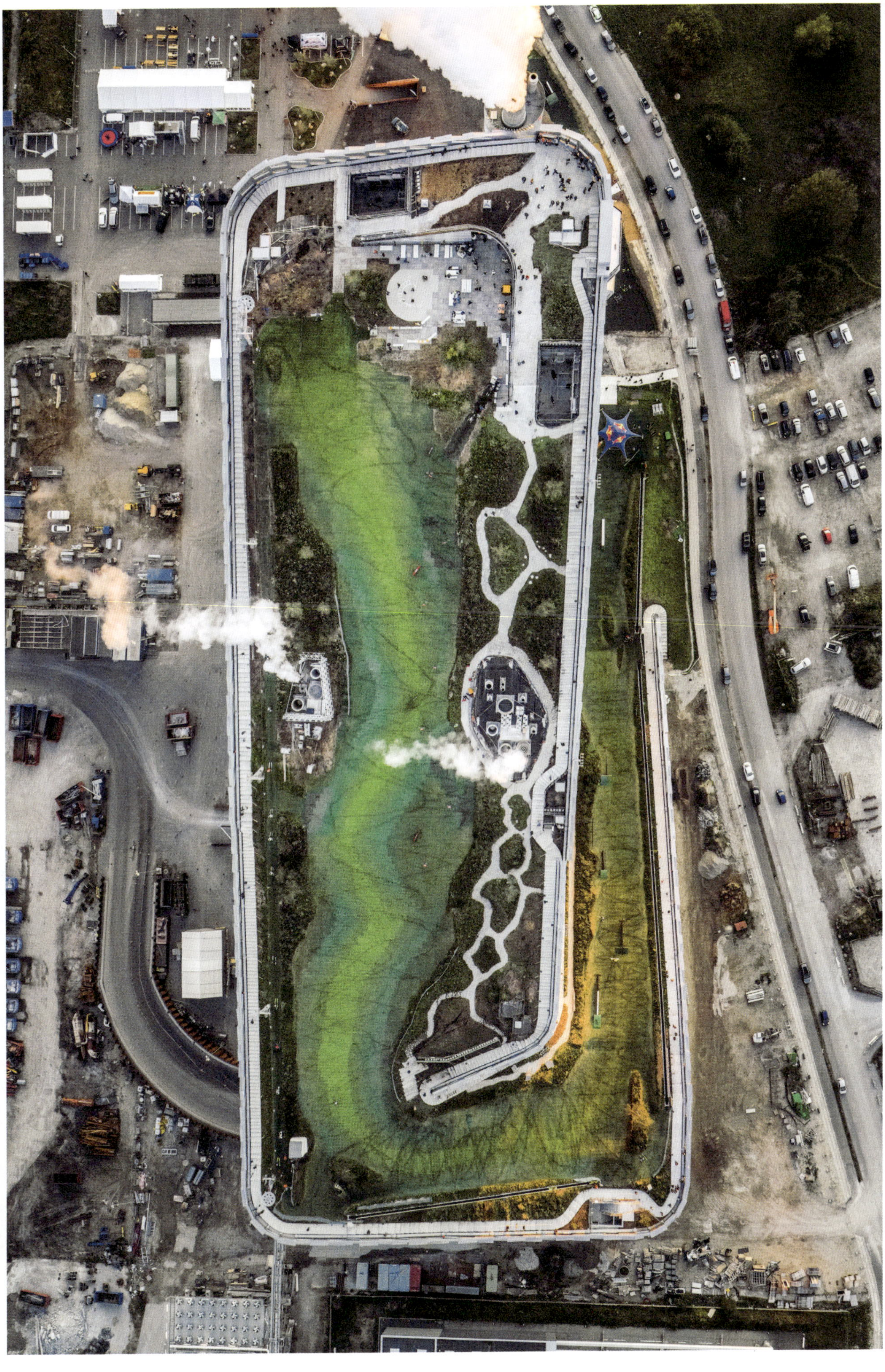

CopenHill, BIG
Copenhagen, Denmark, 2019

Insiders

3 View of CopenHill, both waste-to-energy plant and ski slope, and one of the tallest structures in the city.

97

CopenHill, BIG
Copenhagen, Denmark, 2019

4 A hiking trail up to the top.
5 The building is clad in aluminum bricks, 4 by 10.8 ft. (1.2 by 3.3 m) blocks of rolled aluminum.
6 A skier on the artificial slope.
7 People enjoying the artificial ski slope and recreational hiking area on top of the waste plant.

Insiders 99

Laview Commuter Train, Kazuyo Sejima & Associates
Tokyo and Saitama, Japan, 2019

In 2018 the Seibu Railway company commissioned Tokyo-based architect Kazuyo Sejima, director of Kazuyo Sejima & Associates, to design a limited-express locomotive that would convey the coming of the digital age in transport, as part of the company's centennial celebrations. Sejima conceptualized the project as a moving building and designed the whole train to become a tourist destination in itself, almost like a park where the passenger feels integrated into the scenery both inside and out. The glistening exterior of the cars is made of a semireflective aluminum, so the chameleonic train can reflect its surroundings as it speeds through the Japanese countryside. The interior demonstrates a different approach, with all of the furniture designed by Sejima to be as comfortable as possible. The seating — upholstered in a bright yellow material made in collaboration with Yoko Ando — is designed to feel like that of a living room, creating cocoons of privacy if needed, through high, curved backs and soft cushions. The seating is also capable of rotating so group travelers can face each other. Each passenger has access to the huge windows — the pane falling much lower than in regular commuter trains — that give sweeping views of the surroundings and fill the interior of the cars with natural light.

1 The name *Laview* is an acronym of sorts: L for luxury, a for arrow-like speed, and view because of the train's extralarge windows.
2 The exterior of the train has a reflective sheen.
3 Kazuyo Sejima's design is now a flagship express train for Seibu Railway.

The Mile-Long Opera, Diller Scofidio + Renfro
New York, NY, USA, 2018

1   The High Line was transformed into a thirty-block-long urban stage for the immersive performance.

The Mile-Long Opera, Diller Scofidio + Renfro
New York, NY, USA, 2018

New York-based firm Diller Scofidio + Renfro is known for extending beyond the traditional realm of architecture practice into areas of art, activism, and performance. For eight evenings in October 2018, the High Line — a linear park on a former railway line designed by DS+R in collaboration with Field Operations and Piet Oudoulf — became the site of a spectacular event combining design, music, and poetry. Created by the firm alongside composer David Lang and poets Anne Carson and Claudia Rankine, *The Mile-Long Opera: a biography of 7 o'clock* was an ambulatory operatic experience that explored the changing meaning of that time; the team interviewed dozens of New Yorkers from different backgrounds — including migrant workers, shift workers, and those in complex family units — with their individual stories reflecting a less predictable experience of a time typically associated with security and home. More than one thousand singers from nonprofit organizations and community choirs from the five boroughs of New York were distributed across the entire 1.5-mi. (2.4 km) length of the elevated parkway. Each singer repeated a section of the libretto, so the audience could piece together snatches of harmonized poetry and musings. The result was a work of public art that demonstrated the capacity of an architecture studio to reflect and contribute to the life of a city.

2

2 The city itself was envisioned to be both the opera's subject and backdrop.
3 Some of the more than one thousand singers brought together from across New York were positioned on small podiums.
4 Vocalist were illuminated by multiple lighting techniques, including transparent bags with LED lights inside and these custom-made caps with glowing brims.
5 *The Mile-Long Opera* invited audiences to move in and out of groups of singers as they walked along the High Line.

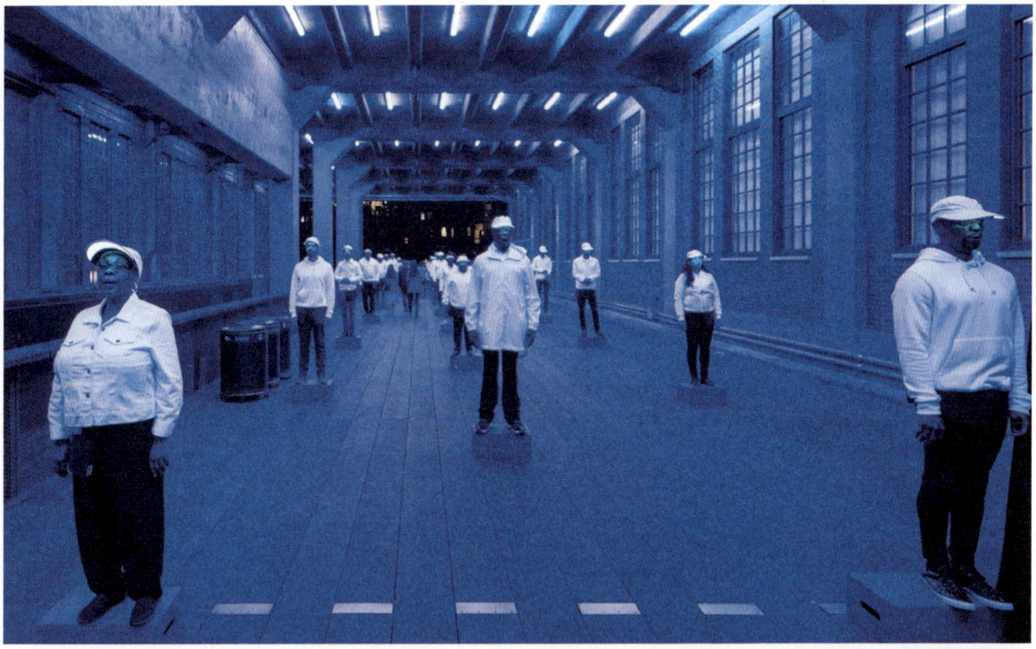
3

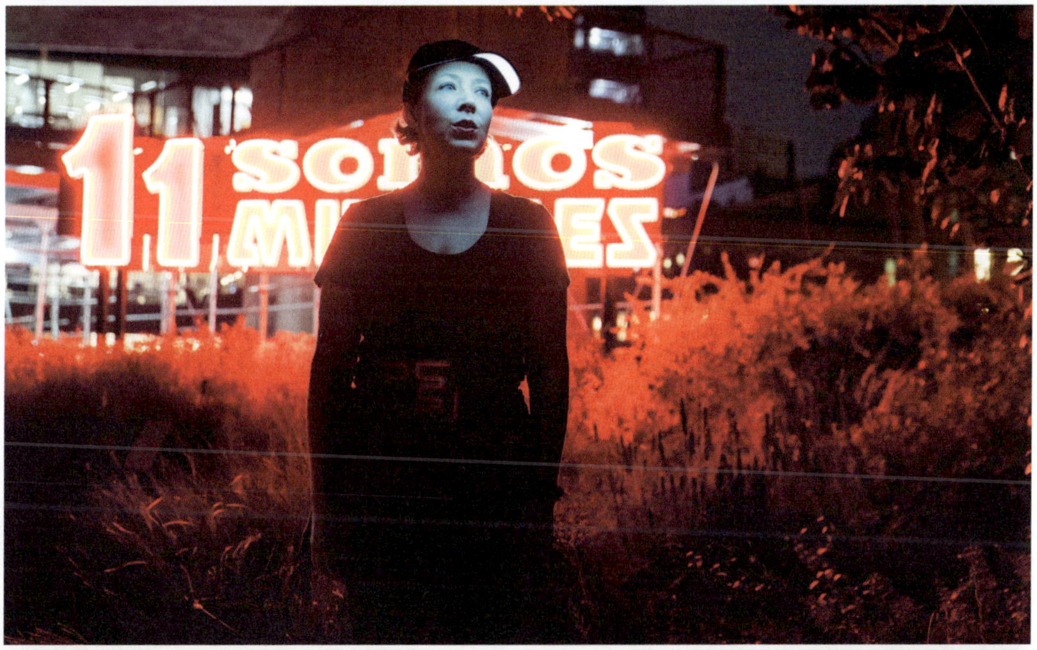
4

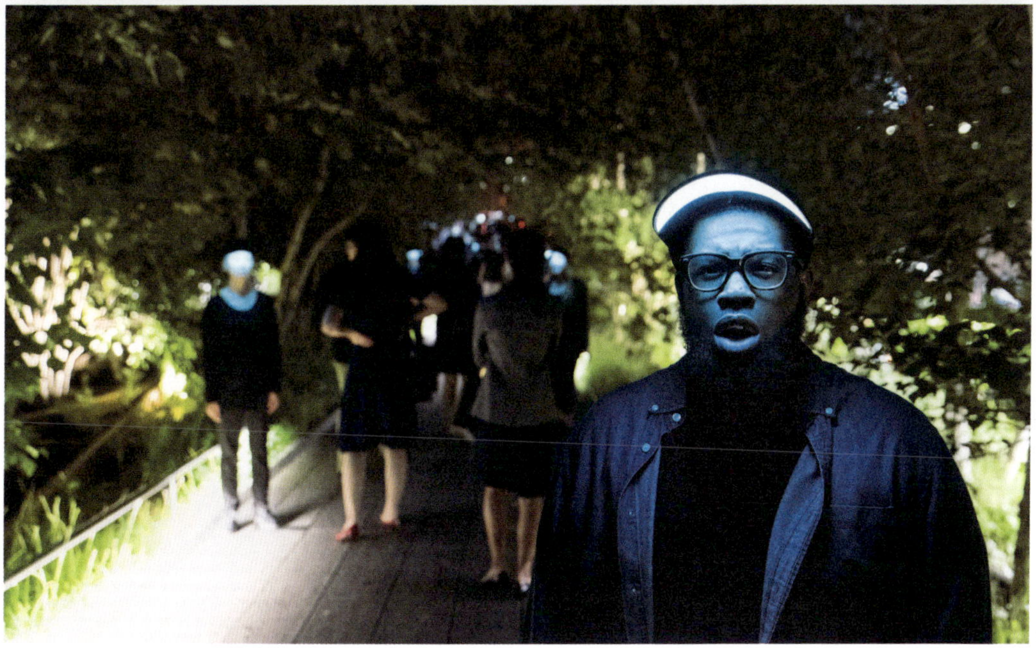
5

THREAD: Artists' Residency and Cultural Center, Toshiko Mori
Sinthian, Senegal, 2015

1 A parametric transformation of the region's traditional pitched roof is achieved through a process of inversion. The bamboo and thatch were harvested nearby by a team of local builders and artisans, thus allowing for ease of repair.
2 The project is situated in the remote community of Sinthian, Senegal, near the border with Mali, a landscape characterized by vast, flat bushland.

In the small village of Sinthian in southeastern Senegal, thatched roofs have never seemed so spectacular. Here, the traditional element is transformed, sweeping in complex double curves over the rammed earth walls of the Toshiko Mori–designed artists' residency and cultural center. The project is the culmination of cultural, academic, and agricultural exchange between high-tech engineering techniques — as seen in the double curvature of the roof — and vernacular design. The building's pitched roof and dense thatch collect and filter rainwater in a system of canals. The water is stored in reservoirs and is used to grow crops during the region's prolonged eight-month dry season. The two large oculi at the heart of the center generate natural ventilation through the "stack effect," as hot air rises and slowly seeps out, keeping the center cool throughout the day and warm in the evening. The gardens that surround the center are managed by a women-led labor collective and used to grow crops, including okra and peanuts, while the spaces inside the center are used for crafts, such as soap making, giving a source of income to participating families. The center also provides connective tissues between community groups who would not usually convene; for example, hosting a health advice service available to the many local tribes that don't have a shared language.

THREAD: Artists' Residency and Cultural Center, Toshiko Mori
Sinthian, Senegal, 2015

3

3   THREAD at dusk. The nighttime lighting is powered by on-site solar panels.
4   The center serves multiple functions for the community, including as an important gathering space.
5   The shared music, art, and performance programs are a testament to the resiliency of the region.
6   The compressed-mud blocks are crafted from earth sourced on-site, while the mosaic floor is made of repurposed ceramic tiles, essentially construction waste from other building work in the region.

4

Insiders 109

The Imaginaries of Transformation, Lacaton & Vassal, Frédéric Druot, and Karine Dana
2015

1. The Grand Parc housing estate encompasses three large blocks of social housing in Bordeaux, France.
2. Small existing windows were replaced by large glazed sliding doors. Winter gardens and balconies were added to the front of each apartment.
3. The 1960s high-rise apartment building before its transformation.

The philosophy of Paris-based architecture firm Lacaton & Vassal, founded by Anne Lacaton and Jean-Philippe Vassal in 1987, is based on a premise that building from the ground up should be a last resort — the firm first seeks to transform existing structures wherever possible. When approaching a renovation project, they have found that 90 percent of the materials needed for the work are nearly always already there. The studio's film *Imaginaries of Transformation*, produced with architect Frédéric Druot and directed by Karine Dana, is a manifesto that challenges a plan by the French government to demolish the long-vilified 1960s Cité du Grand Parc public housing estate in Bordeaux. The architects also put their philosophies to the test by transforming other Modernist housing projects in Saint-Nazaire and Paris. At each site, the architects opened up cramped and badly lit apartments and invented improved ways of using spaces, including interventions such as new elevators, upgraded plumbing, and augmenting existing views across the city. The film documents what the experience for residents of their homes was like before, during, and after each building renovation. It demonstrates the studio's foundational idea: sometimes real innovation comes from preventing the egregious waste of demolition and working cleverly with what is already there.

Housing +, Tatiana Bilbao
Ciudad Acuña, Mexico, 2016

1

2

Mexico has one of the highest population growth rates in Latin America, and its housing shortage currently stands at nine million homes. In 2015, Mexican-born architect Tatiana Bilbao grew concerned that, since the 1990s, the issue of social housing in Mexico has been mainly left to commercial developers, with architects not involved in any substantial way. She perceived that leading designers and academics in the country had been so focused on remaking Mexico's international image as a successful neoliberal economy that the fundamental human right to housing had been neglected for the country's poorest people.[3] Bilbao conducted more than two thousand interviews and held particularized public workshops with people who live in social housing around the country, determining priorities and budgets, and eventually developed a housing system that could be built for $8,000. The opportunity to make it came after a tornado ripped through the northern city of Los Altos de Santa Teresa, which borders with Texas, leaving twenty-three families homeless and in need of emergency housing. The simple design has a central core of concrete blocks, with surrounding modules made from affordable wooden pallets. The first phase of each house includes two bedrooms, one bathroom, one kitchen, and a living room; when completed, the third phase will allow for an additional five bedrooms. With this modular system, Bilbao has created an affordable, expandable construction.

1 Housing + addresses the social housing crisis in Mexico.
2 Homes are modeled on the design of an archetypal house, featuring, for example, a gabled roof.
3 The houses maintain the outside appearance of completed houses while each interior phase is completed.

Insiders

Teopanzolco Cultural Center, Isaac Broid and Productora
Cuernavaca, Mexico, 2017

1 The contemporary cultural center is on a site facing the archeological zone of Teopanzolco.
2 The lobby is placed exactly opposite the pyramid, becoming a vantage point as well as a space to meet before and after events.
3 The building is organized around two elements, with the triangular volume containing the public programs.

Situated opposite the archeological zone of Teopanzolco, the site of the ruins of a double Aztec pyramid, this cultural center is an intelligent and powerful response to its context. Mexico City–based firm Productora, working with Isaac Broid, paid visual homage to the Mesoamerican civilization with a wide, stepped pyramidal structure. The site presented a unique opportunity to establish not only a formal dialogue with the ancient structure, but also a cultural one. Working with a restrained palette combining deep ochre-tinted concrete with wood and oxidized steel, the architects created five different environments. In addition to a nine-hundred-seat concert hall, the center features a theater for experimental performances and a lobby that is used for chamber concerts. A second, small open-air theater surrounds the building; this plinth also incorporates a series of patios and gardens, as well as a number of existing trees. Perhaps the most inventive space is the roof, which dips to ground level on the side facing the ruins of the double pyramid and slopes upward in a series of wide steps that lead up to the highest point of the structure. The landscaping, while sparse, incorporates preexisting trees.

Pearling Site Museum and entrance, Valerio Olgiati
Muharraq, Bahrain, 2019

1

116

The oyster beds on the northern shores of Bahrain were the heart of a pearling industry that dominated the Gulf from the third century to the early twentieth century CE. Before the discovery of oil and gas that initiated a radical transformation of the region, nearly everyone in the city of Muharraq was directly involved in the discovery and export of its prized pearls. The surviving traces of this heritage are now the subject of an expansive master-planning and regeneration initiative, as well as a tourist route, that puts contemporary architecture and design at its core. The 2.2-mi. (3.5 km) Pearling Path takes visitors past three oyster beds, a seashore site, and historically significant structures, with the goal of reconnecting the island with its heritage, as a marker of a cultural identity that had nearly disappeared. To serve as a catalyst for urban revitalization, it is also an urban trail, bridging the coastline to the city. For the visitor center, Swiss architect Valerio Olgiati conceived a roof structure of a 32.8-ft.-high (10 m) earthy concrete canopy — uniting disparate historic buildings beneath — pierced by towers and apertures. Olgiati created new forms of public space, such as a shelter with apertures to the sky, while preserving what remains of an original pearling warehouse. The building now gives a context to the ruins and hosts workshops and exhibitions for tourists, and events for the local community.

1   The concrete canopy of the Pearling Path Center creates a new public space for the ancient city of Muharraq, Bahrain, and fits into a master plan for the UNESCO World Heritage site.

Pearling Site Museum and entrance, Valerio Olgiati
Muharraq, Bahrain, 2019

2 A large space is created in which a forest of columns and wind towers hold the horizontal canopy above ground.
3 The site contains ruins that form part of the Pearling Path.
4 The sweeping canopy provides vital shade for the local community in the very hot climate of Muharraq.
5 Interior view of the Pearling Site Museum lounge area.

Insiders 119

A Dead Forest for the Trojan Women, Stefano Boeri Architetti
Syracuse, Italy, 2019

Stefano Boeri's career has spanned numerous modes of engagement with architecture, from design to criticism and exhibition-making, as well as politics. His eponymous architecture studio is responsible for the design of the Bosco Verticale, or Vertical Forest, residential towers that feature facades teeming with trees and plant life. Boeri's multifaceted career highlights the complexity of architectural training today. When invited to design a scenography for a retelling of the ancient Greek tragedy *The Trojan Women* by Euripides in an outdoor amphitheater in Sicily, the architect took the opportunity to make a powerful commentary on a recent environmental catastrophe. An unprecedented hurricane with violent winds had decimated many forests in northeastern Italy, felling thousands of trees that were sprawled across the landscape. In memory of these remains of cypress and maritime pines, Boeri positioned 250 bare trunks, supported by a simple metal structure, in rows like resurrected soldiers. The arrangement underscored the toll of the recent disaster and reflected on the destruction in the homelands of the Trojan women — the play's protagonists — who themselves were symbolic of current-day refugees moving through Italy. The stark forms of the tree trunks served as the backdrop for the play, set in the classical geometry of the ancient stone Teatro Greco stage, before being donated to the local timber industry as production material.

1 Fallen trees in the Carnic Alps in northeastern Italy in the wake of storm Vaia. Destruction at this scale had never been seen before in this region, and the disaster was attributed to extreme weather patterns caused by climate change.
2 The performance was set in the ancient Greek amphitheater in Syracuse, Italy, with 250 dead trees employed in the scenography.

radicals

The artists, writers, researchers, and filmmakers in this chapter pollinate multiple spaces, propagating ideas and visions in fertile ground. While few in this group might identify their work as architecture, each project here illuminates new knowledge about our current and future world. Electrifying still and moving images show little-known industrial and postindustrial rural and city landscapes; share complex, empowering stories about racial identity; and provide chilling glimpses of our imminent futures. The practitioners in this chapter see architecture as a medium that can be used, revised, explored, then abstracted and activated again through sculpture, painting, and documentation. For example, a significant public space in Italy is shrouded in the remains of jute sacks from Ghana, giving physical form to the invisible but powerful systems of empire that still govern the movement of goods and people. A painter, sculptor, and production designer use stories of real and imaginary cities to reflect on and critique consequential historical events. Spatial practitioners are also activists, breaking out of the institution and into the city, or breaking out of the city and into the rainforest. They ask what is the space of sound, or what is the body that is formed by architecture, and answer with extraordinary vision. These radical thinkers are part of a thriving culture that analyzes the post-occupancy role of architecture as it inhabits the city and works both for and against lives and communities — positing the idea that it is people and systems who really make a city, rather than simply built structures. Through this lens, this set of practitioners are detecting, distilling, and disseminating the important spatial and social issues of our time.

Feedlots, Mishka Henner
2012–13

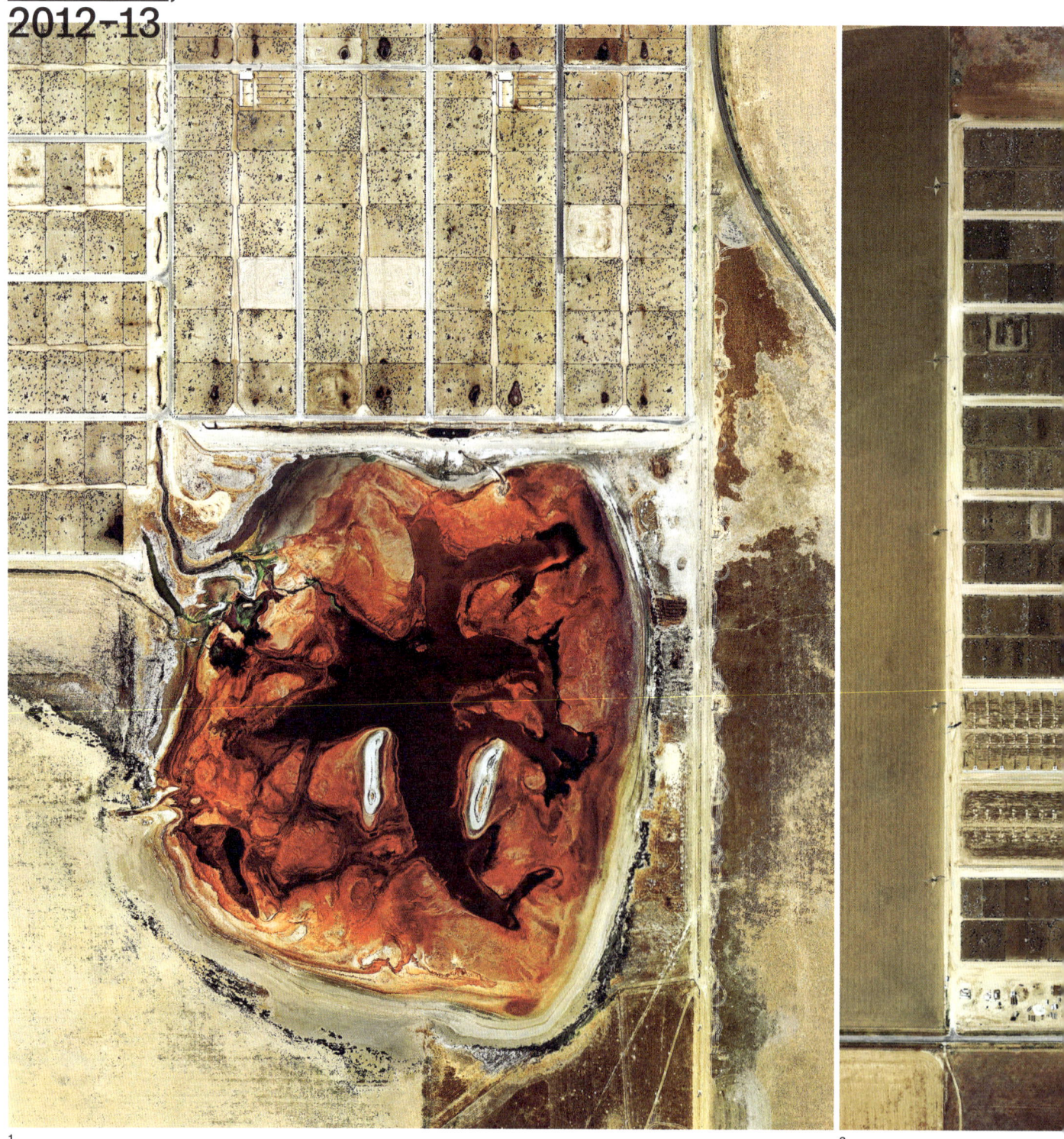

Food production takes up almost 40 percent of habitable land on this planet. Despite this startling figure, very few of us can accurately visualize the spatial realities of industrial agriculture. Manchester, UK–based artist Mishka Henner's profound and memorable photography series *Feedlots* is sure to correct that. The large-scale photographs depict gridded acres of arid land in Texas adjacent to luridly beautiful lagoons. It is only on close inspection that the black dots peppering the images become identifiable as individual cattle, and the brightly colored lakes are revealed to be cesspools of raw animal waste being treated by highly polluting chemicals. Feedlots like these are standard in the United States. The photos reveal how 99 percent of livestock production in the country is kept and maintained; this is where meat comes from. The photographs, which Henner stitched together from available high-resolution satellite imagery of the area, offer viewers the opportunity to question their complicity in this harrowing system of industrial animal production, central to the way that many people live. The feedlots' design systems offer visual evidence of the key factors that are involved: feedlots maximize land use, increase the weight of the animals, and reduce their life span. Beyond the moral implications regarding the animals' welfare, Henner also presents the environmental catastrophe — poisonous lakes and the effect on surrounding water systems — for consideration.

Radicals

1 *Coronado Feeders, Dalhart, Texas, 2012.*
2 *Wrangler Feedyard, Tulia, Texas, 2013.*

Feedlots, Mishka Henner
2012–13

3   *Tascosa Feedyard, Bushland, Texas* (detail), 2012.

The Proposal, Jill Magid
2018

Mexican architect Luis Barragán is revered for his Modern buildings and forms that play with bright colors, light, volume, and nature. When he died in 1988, his archive of drawings, models, and photographs, as well as their copyright, was acquired by an independent collector, the CEO of Swiss furniture-manufacturing company Vitra, who gave the cache of documents to his future wife as an engagement gift. Since then, the archives have been maintained by Vitra, which strictly enforces their rights over the material. When Brooklyn–based artist Jill Magid experienced the challenges to accessing the archive firsthand, she began questioning why the archive was not housed in a site accessible to the public in Mexico. Magid's controversial feature documentary *The Proposal* chronicles her quest to destabilize the status of the archive. In it, she offers an engagement ring set with a two-carat rough-cut diamond grown from a fraction of Barragán's ashes — which Magid had exhumed in Guadalajara with permission from Barragán's family and the Mexican government — in exchange for the archive's repatriation to Mexico from Switzerland. Through a series of actions and artworks, she galvanized Barragán's descendants and the Mexican government around the project, also receiving support from international arts institutions, attorneys, architecture critics, and writers. The radical, and arguably romantic, deal Magid proposed has not yet been accepted; however, the project did provoke debate over public access, ownership, and the control of works of national heritage.

1   Jill Magid, *The Proposal* (detail, ring), 2016. 2.02 carat, blue, uncut, diamond, ring box, documents.
2   Jill Magid, *The Proposal*, 2018. Feature documentary, 83 minutes.

HOWL, eon (I, II), Julie Mehretu
San Francisco, CA, USA, 2017

New York–based artist Julie Mehretu's abstract paintings and drawings often refer to elements of mapping and architecture, achieving a calligraphic complexity that resembles turbulent atmospheres and dense social networks. Her large-scale paintings engage the history of nonobjective art from Constructivism to Futurism, posing questions about the relationship between utopian impulses and abstraction. HOWL, eon (I, II) is a site-specific commission for the San Francisco Museum of Modern Art, in which Mehretu recontextualizes the history of American landscape painting through depicting layers of social activity. She references the ways that landscapes have been politicized through historical events in the United States — from the violent expansion of the American West to colonialism, abolition, and sites of social unrest. The manipulated digital images in the underpainting of HOWL, eon (I, II) refer to the large abstract paintings of the American expansion, with direct references to Frederic Edwin Church and Thomas Cole. Air-brushed color, screen printed squares, and ink brush strokes on the paintings' surfaces allude to contemporary race riots, street protests, and nineteenth-century depictions of the city. The abstract gestures and erasures reflect a landscape continually reshaped by physical movement and struggle, reminding us of the conjoined genealogies of chaos, exploitation, and ambition in the making of the American West.

1 Julie Mehretu transformed a decommissioned church in the New York City neighborhood of Harlem into her temporary studio in order to make her towering work.
2 HOWL, eon (I), 2017.

Moriyama-San, Bêka & Lemoine
2017

Ila Bêka and Louise Lemoine have transformed the representation of contemporary architecture through their films. The productions do not focus on explaining the buildings' structure, design, and technical details but instead let the viewer share in an intimate, invisible bubble of daily life. Through a series of moments and fragmented scenes, an unusually spontaneous architectural portrait of the home and the inhabitants emerges. The series includes the iconic *Koolhaas Houselife* (2008), for example, which follows a housekeeper as she spends her days in and around a 1998 Rem Koolhaas–designed home in Bordeaux, France. In *Moriyama-San* the filmmakers invites viewers to glimpse into the life of the owner of the Moriyama House. Designed in 2005 by Ryue Nishizawa, cofounder of architecture firm SANAA, the building is one of the most significant contemporary houses in Japan. The sequence of ten white volumes — the architecture as a whole creating a complex streetscape — was designed to give the owner a unique habitat suited to his way of living. The soulful and witty film spends a week exploring the endearing, eccentric, and enigmatic character and routines of the hermit-like owner, Yasuo Moriyama, as well as demonstrating a radical, visionary new way of living and being in space.

1 The film captures one week in the extraordinary-ordinary life of Yasuo Moriyama.
2 Moriyama tending to his garden.
3 An urban hermit, Moriyama lives in an archipelago of peace and contemplation in the heart of Tokyo.
4 The house is segmented into ten individual blocks, ranging from one to three stories and punctured by large windows.

Moriyama-San, Bêka & Lemoine
2017

5

5 The filmmakers filmed Moriyama as he went about his usual activities, including reading, listening to records, and caring for the garden.
6 Moriyama reading.
7 The film celebrates Moriyama's love for noise music, a passion he shares with the filmmakers.
8 Moriyama napping in front of an Armless chair (also known as the Rabbit Ear chair), which SANAA designed for Nextmaruni.

6

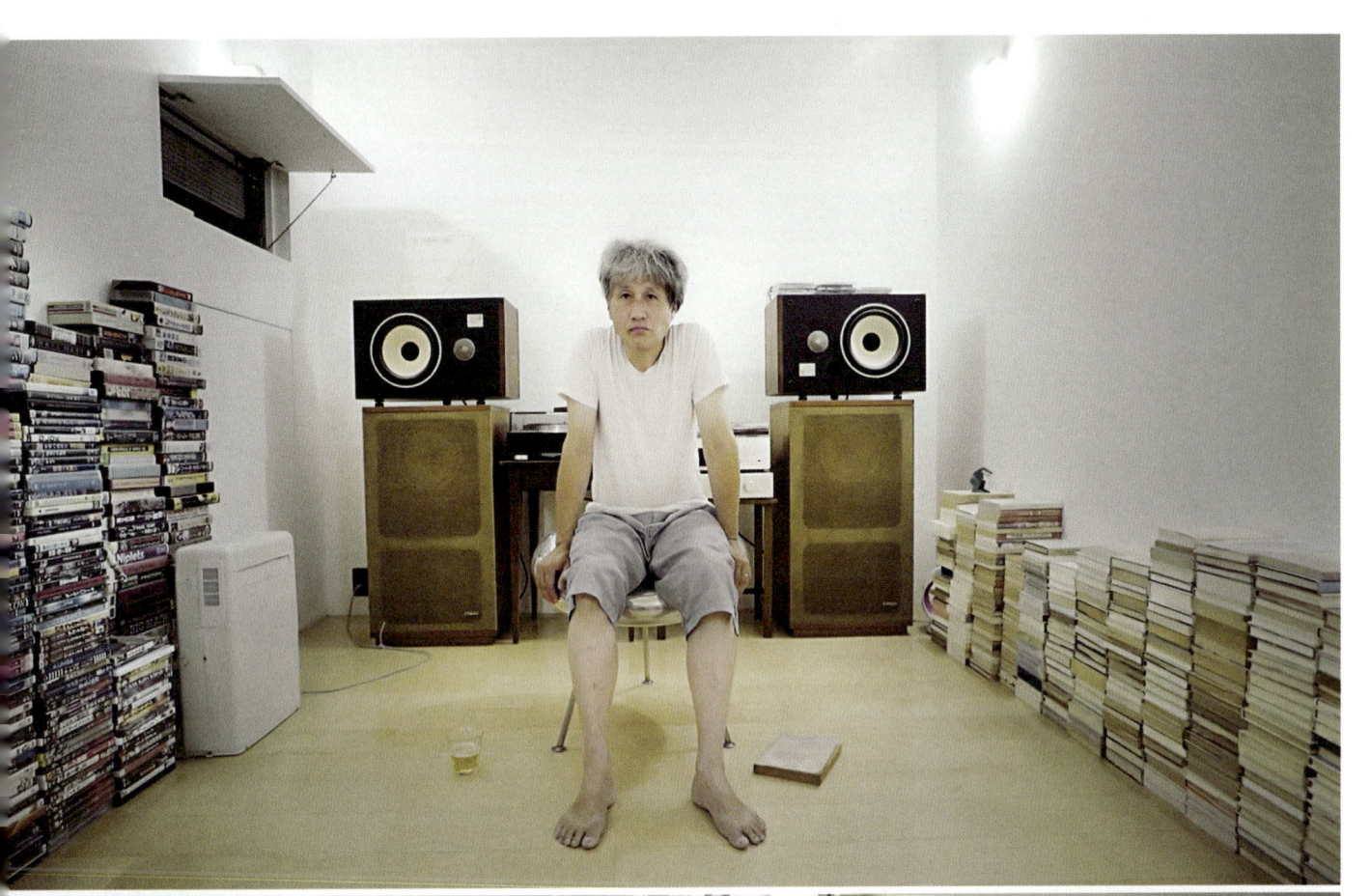

Radicals

Western Flag (Spindletop, Texas) 2017, John Gerrard 2017

Western Flag is a hyperrealistic digital simulation by Irish artist John Gerrard set in the barren and depleted plains of Spindletop, Texas, on what was once the Lucas gusher, the site of the world's first great oil rush in 1901. That discovery was a starting gun in the global race for oil that transformed the Western economy in the twentieth century, as well as the beginning of irreversible planetary-scale environmental catastrophes we see now in the twenty-first. The mesmerizing moving image shows a single flagpole perpetually pumping high-pressurized black smoke into the atmosphere as the camera slowly orbits around. The work operates in parallel to the real passage of time in Spindletop, so the sun rises and sets, the moon waxes and wanes as the hours and days change in real time. This exacting and elaborate re-creation and forensic manipulation of space, time, sound, and air is fundamental to the power of Gerrard's spatial and environmental works. He begins with a detailed photographic survey of the site, then engages computer programmers, modelers, and video game designers to meticulously construct astonishingly real virtual worlds. Every one of the frames of the installation is unique and jnot recycled, meaning that the work is close in spirit to a live transmission of a site, the exact moments of which can never be re-created.

1 Simulation still from *Western Flag (Spindletop, Texas), 2017*, showing the flagpole bearing a flag of perpetually renewing pressurized black smoke.
2 Simulation still from *Western Flag (Spindletop, Texas), 2017*, at sunrise.
3 *Western Flag (Spindletop, Texas), 2017*, installation view, Somerset House, London, 2017.

Radicals

Flint Is Family Part I, LaToya Ruby Frazier
2016–17

One of the most severe man-made environmental catastrophes in the history of the United States happened in Flint, Michigan, a struggling postindustrial city in the Rust Belt. The city's economically motivated decision in 2014 to switch its water supply caused irreversible damage to infrastructure, leaving the predominantly working-class residents with toxic lead-laced water contaminated by deadly legionella bacteria, which led to suffering, sickness, exhaustion, and death. Artist, photographer, activist, and advocate LaToya Ruby Frazier examines this story of environmental justice, human rights violations, and disinvestment in *Flint Is Family Part I*, a photography series of intimate collaborative portraits and video of the Cobb family as they navigate the crisis; her portraits depict the family negotiating daily tasks of cooking, cleaning, brushing their teeth, and bathing using bottled water. Building on her previous work in documentary photography exploring identities of place, race, and family, Frazier positions these portraits within a wider series depicting decades of institutional and corporate abuse that have transformed Flint, along with other once-booming steel, car, lumber, and similar manufacturing cities, into ghost towns. Money from the sale of these photographs funded an atmospheric water generator, which now provides free clean water to Flint residents. In *Flint Is Family Part I*, Frazier reveals the power of photographs as tools for justice.

1   *Students and residents outside Northwestern High School (est. 1964) awaiting the arrival of President Barack Obama, May 4th 2016, III, 2016–17.*
2   *Shea doing crochet braids in her cousin Andrea's hair for Andrea's daughter's wedding, 2016–17.*
3   *Students and residents outside Northwestern High School (est. 1964) awaiting the arrival of President Barack Obama, May 4th 2016, II, 2016–17.*
4   *The Grainery Natural Grocer Signage on the corner of E. Court and Church St., 2016–17.*

Radicals

Flint is Family Part I, LaToya Ruby Frazier
2016–17

5 City of Flint Water Plant and the Industrial Iron & Metal Co., 2016–17.
6 Shea Cobb with her daughter, Zion, and her mother, Ms. Renée, outside the Social Network banquet hall, 2016.

Radicals

Asia One, Cao Fei
2018

As a teenager in southern China in the 1990s, artist Cao Fei observed the opening up of her country to the West, watching as once-quiet provinces transformed into the factories of the world. An early user of immersive computer game Second Life, Cao spent thousands of hours building her own online world named RMB City, a condensed, satirical incarnation of contemporary Chinese cities in the popular imagination at that time. It was a constantly updating island composed of "Made in China" souvenirs, including generic skyscrapers, bicycle wheels, shipping containers, and shopping malls, as well as Rem Koolhaas's iconic CCTV tower. For her multimedia installation *Asia One*, Cao's interest in artificial worlds melds with reality. Filmed in Shanghai at the first fully automated postal-distribution center, run entirely by AI technology, her project follows the immersion of China's post-'90s generation (which was born into the strict one-child policy and grew up as China's economy was booming) in digital networks and virtual environments. The narrative arc of the video tracks the life of the company's transparently inessential human employees, the purposeless workers moving throughout the empty sorting center. Cao is fascinated by the rich and fantastical inner worlds of seemingly hopeless individuals;[4] she ponders the alienating effect of rapid urbanization, advanced technology, and surveillance on the psyche of a generation.

1

1 The two protagonists of *Asia One*, set inside a package distribution center.
2 One protagonist rides a conveyor belt as if she were a product.
3 A giant octopus adds an element of fantasy to *Asia One*.
4 The protagonist rests her head, watched over by a plastic android.

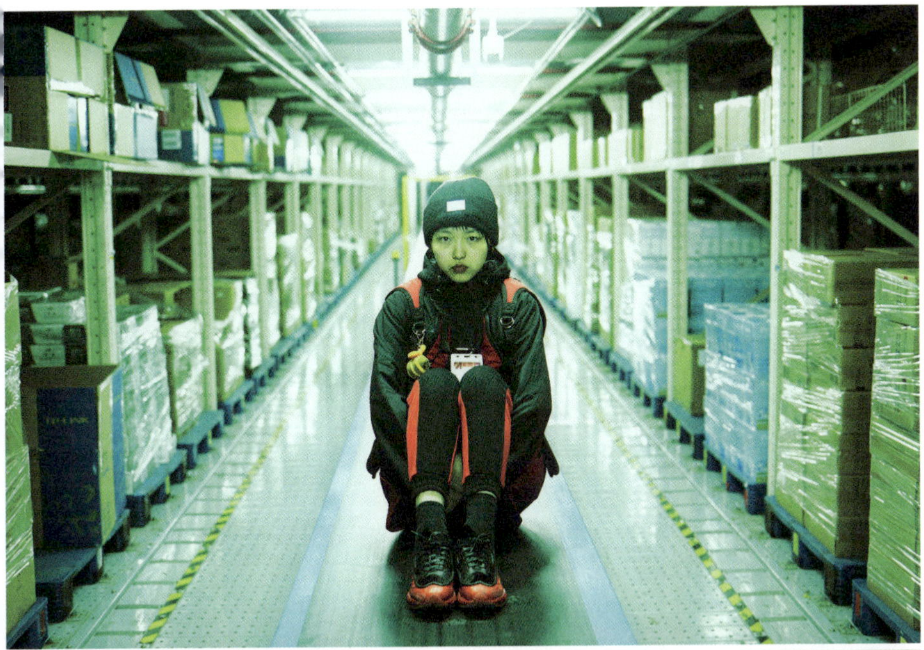

2

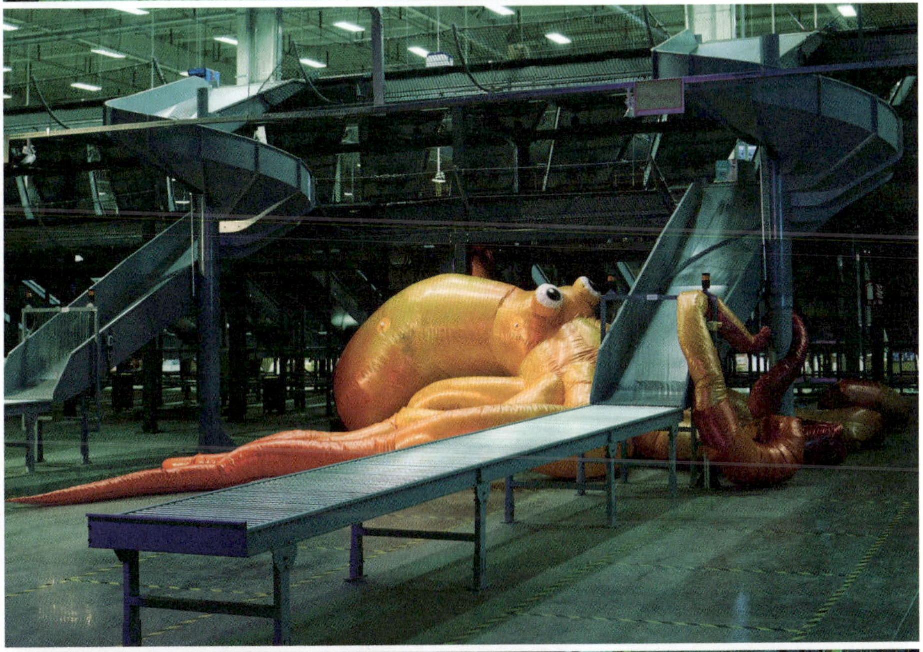

3

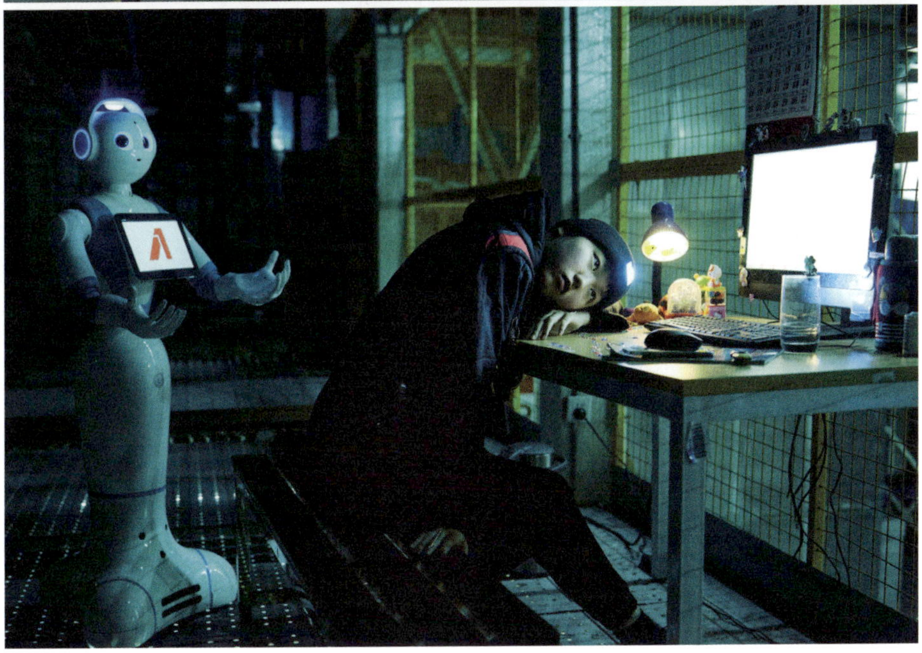

4

Pro-EU / Anti-Brexit Campaign, Wolfgang Tillmans 2016

As is the situation for many European artists, Wolfgang Tillmans' career was forged in a time when traveling across the continent for periods of work and education was encouraged and enabled by the European Union. In the early 1990s he studied at Bournemouth and Poole College of Art, and called London home for twenty-six years. He was the first non-British-born artist to both win the Turner Prize and become a member of the Royal Academy of Arts. When the United Kingdom's Brexit referendum was announced by the government in February 2016, the British public was invited to vote whether to "leave" the EU or "remain" — retaining existing privileges of living and working across any of the member states. Tillmans, himself a "remainer," perceived the Britain Stronger in Europe campaign, which included members from across the political spectrum, as lackluster. From his studios in Berlin and London, Tillmans began exploring ways to establish a grassroots pro-European statement. Layering his own photographs — depictions of the British coastline, Glastonbury music festival, hazy sunrises — with emotive messages, he created posters that were available to download from his website for people to print out or share on social media. The imagery was also pasted by supporters on scaffolding across the UK. In the end, the campaign's success was not matched by the result, but the strategy remains a fascinating and poignant effort to hold together the European project.

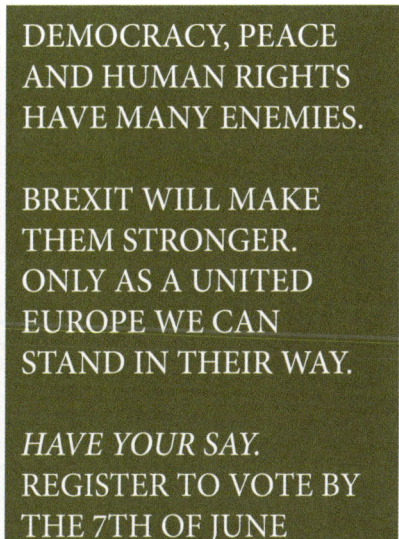

1 Wolfgang Tillmans' anti-Brexit campaign posters pasted on the side of Photo London's annual pavilion situated in the Edmond J. Safra Fountain Court of Somerset House in London.
2 A selection of Tillmans's anti-Brexit campaign posters.

Radicals

143

The invisible enemy should not exist, Michael Rakowitz
London, England, UK, 2018

In the mid-1970s, Iraq was producing three-quarters of the world's dates, its second-biggest export after oil. The country's thirty million date trees were famous in the Middle East; their palm leaves and fruits are a distinctive presence in ancient Assyrian architecture and art. After decades of invasion and war, the date trees, approximately three million of which are left, and their syrup, which is now subject to stringent sanctions on exports, have become a weather vane for the demise and decimation of Iraqi culture. Their story is at the center of this multilayered sculpture by Iraqi American artist Michael Rakowitz. Situated on the fourth plinth in London's Trafalgar Square, it is pointedly positioned to face toward the Houses of Parliament, where the decision to go to war against Iraq was made. The work is a full-scale replica of a sculpture of the ancient winged protective deity lamassu, which had guarded the Nergal Gate of Nineveh since 700 BCE, until the so-called Islamic State destroyed it in 2015. The sculpture's colored metal form is made from thousands of tins of Iraqi date syrup. The origin of the food packaging is veiled, because of the sanctions; Rakowitz's "ghost"[5] of ancient Assyrian sculpture reflects on the power structures of culture and strives to materialize what was lost.

1   The inscription — written in cuneiform, one of the earliest systems of writing — says, "Sennacherib, king of the world, king of Assyria, had the inner and outer wall of Nineveh built anew and raised as high as mountains."
2   The lamassu, a winged bull with a human face, is made from more than ten thousand empty Iraqi date syrup cans.

Love is the Message, The Message is Death, Arthur Jafa
2016

Arthur Jafa addresses the prismatic complexity of Black identity in the United States in this seven-minute film that splices representations of charisma, talent, and beauty with tense and desperate scenes of historical and present-day poverty, violence, and injustice. Slipping between subjects, Jafa collages his archive of found footage — the film tightly choreographs its way through the schizophrenic landscape of a country that openly idolizes and imitates Black athletes, Black music, Black celebrity, and denigrates and systematically underserves Black people. Jafa, an artist, film director, and cinematographer, drills into the minutiae of media representation of African Americans' lives, in an age when almost everything can be recorded. Within just a few seconds, he cuts from clips of LeBron James's slam dunk to the aftermath of Hurricane Katrina, the opening seconds of President Obama's spontaneous 2015 rendition of "Amazing Grace," a civil rights march, and bodies dancing, all to the emotive and tender soundtrack of Kanye West's gospel hip-hop song "Ultralight Beam." The work offers no hierarchies or narrative, generating instead an emotional, almost haptic relationship with its audience as it ricochets between scenes of trauma and joy, distance and intimacy. In the summer of 2020, in the midst of a global Black Lives Matter movement, thirteen US– and European–based art museums collaborated to make the video work available online for forty-eight hours.

1 *Love is the Message, The Message is Death*, 2016, installation view, Museum of Contemporary Art, Los Angeles.
2 Video still from Arthur Jafa's work depicting a scene from the 1963 March on Washington for Jobs and Freedom held in Washington, DC.

Black Panther, Hannah Beachler
2018

1   Concept sketch by Till Nowak showing the conical skyscrapers that comprise Wakanda's capital, the Golden City, with T'Challa's palace in the foreground.
2   The Kingdom of Wakanda is designed to be the most advanced nation on planet Earth. In this concept sketch by Nowak, the Golden City — while a fantasy — is still recognizable as a terrestrial city.
3   Concept sketch by Nowak for the Jabari Lands, showing an intricately made wooden city built from trees growing at the base of the mountain.

The 1970s comic book *Black Panther* was tapped by Marvel Studios in early 2014 to serve as the basis for the next big super hero movie in the Marvel Cinematic Universe. Featuring a predominantly Black cast, the film called for the design of a fictional nation in Africa, called Wakanda, that had hidden from the rest of the world's view for hundreds of years. As planet Earth's most high-tech country, Wakanda was built from its own supply of "vibranium," the most powerful substance in existence. In designing and building this fantasy country for the film, production designer Hannah Beachler began by examining the native tribal culture of the countries of Senegal, Uganda, and Kenya and imagined how countries such as these might have evolved had they never been colonized, instead surpassing the rest of the world technologically. Beachler felt it was important to imbue all Wakandans with a sense of belonging; her design process began with a timeline of the history of the fictional country. While the rest of the Earth's societies were in the Industrial Revolution, Wakanda already had technologically sophisticated communications and advanced transit, art, and agriculture. Beachler's landscape evolved through a heterogeneous layering of designs, from nineteenth-century warehouses to edifices inspired by the work of architect Zaha Hadid.

Year 3, Steve McQueen
London, England, UK, 2019

The annual class photo is an ingrained ritual in England. Families preserve the photographs year after year as a record of their children's changing heights, hairstyles, and best friends. Artist and film director Steve McQueen chose Year 3 (the UK equivalent of second grade) as the subject of a work so ambitious that it took on the scope of a city. Every Year 3 class in London was invited to have its photograph taken for the artist — a total of more than seventy-six thousand children participated. The images of classes of around twenty to thirty seven-year-olds in their various school uniforms or in casual dress were framed and installed on the walls of Tate Britain as a large-scale installation, as well as blown up and posted on billboards all over the city. The photographs, with the kids grinning proudly at the camera, occupied non-art spaces: a bridge, a highway, the side of shops, and advertising displays on Tube platforms. In its scale it was a portrait of a city like no other. The age of seven holds a fascination for McQueen because this is the age when children start to understand issues of race, gender, and class. At a time when the UK was finalizing its exit from the European Union, which most of the city voted against, the message McQueen seems to send is that this capital is not isolated, homogenous, or insular — its future is wide open.

1

1 *Year 3* billboard at Caledonian Road, Islington in London.
2 A neighboring *Year 3* billboard at Caledonian Road, Islington in London.
3 *Year 3* billboard at Belsize Road, Camden in London.
4 *Year 3* billboard at Ilderton Road, Lewisham in London.

2

3

4

A Friend, Ibrahim Mahama
Milan, Italy, 2019

Living and working in Accra, Kumasi, and Tamale, Ghanaian artist and writer Ibrahim Mahama engages in the forming of architectural spaces inspired by the promise and failure of the Modernist movement. His art practice started as a way of expressing his interest in the history of materials and architecture. His large-scale site-specific installation *A Friend* — commissioned and produced by Fondazione Nicola Trussardi — stopped people in their tracks when it took over ancient tollgates of Porta Venezia, in the center of Milan. Mahama's temporary monument transformed what was historically a threshold of the city, a point of crossing, into a space to pause. As he frequently does in his work, the artist used a specific material — in this case over ten thousand worn jute sacks — to become manifestations of forgotten or unsung modes of production and material goods. Fabricated in China, Bangladesh, or India, the sacks are then imported by the Ghana Cocoa Board to transport cocoa beans and eventually end up as multifunctional objects, used for the transportation of food, charcoal, and other commodities. At the point of almost total decay, they are sewn together by Mahama's network of collaborators and then superimposed onto architecture. The bags are printed with import stamps and branding as they move from place to place — these various records of checkpoints and travel are mapped onto the ancient gates, underlining the trafficking of people and goods in society.

1   View of the site-specific installation conceived for the two neoclassical tollgates of Porta Venezia.
2   The gateway remains one of Milan's most prominent landmarks, bordering the many multiethnic neighborhoods that surround it today.
3   Detail of the jute sacks used to wrap Porta Venezia.
4   The artist created a second skin and new identity for the two structures.

2

3

4

The Institute of Isolation, Lucy McRae
2016

1 A still from *The Institute of Isolation*, an observational documentary that contemplates whether isolation, and extreme experience, might be used as a gateway to training human resilience. Shown here is the microgravity trainer.

The Institute of Isolation, Lucy McRae
2016

Sci-fi artist and body architect Lucy McRae's otherworldly films focus on examining the relationship of the human body to space. Her work — which also takes the form of photography and installation — imagines ways in which design, architecture, performance, and even biological adaptation could change and alter fundamental aspects of the human body; she offers speculative scenarios that question exactly what radical transformations our bodies may need to undertake in order to survive. Set in a near-future reality, The Institute of Isolation is a short film about a desolate fictional research and training center filled with devices, training equipment, and architectural conditions that could make human bodies capable of surviving in outer space. A series of sensory chambers challenge the body and brain to adapt, while a microgravity trainer allows the film's protagonist to prepare for space. These sites are used to probe the role buildings could have in altering human biology on an evolutionary scale. McRae selected several sites of extreme architecture and design as shooting locations, with scenes set in Spanish radical architect Ricardo Bofill's La Fábrica house in Barcelona, as well as large public spaces, including the Royal Botanic Gardens, Kew in London.

2 An elevated walkway at the Royal Botanic Gardens, Kew in London in use as part of the fictional research and training ground for the Institute of Isolation.
3 A storage container for earplugs — a prop from the film — photographed on architect Ricardo Bofill's cutting mat.
4 The film's protagonist departing the Temperate House (1862) — the largest surviving Victorian glasshouse in the world — at the Royal Botanic Gardens, Kew.
5 The protagonist shown inside a hyperbaric chamber at the LKH University Hospital in Graz, Austria.

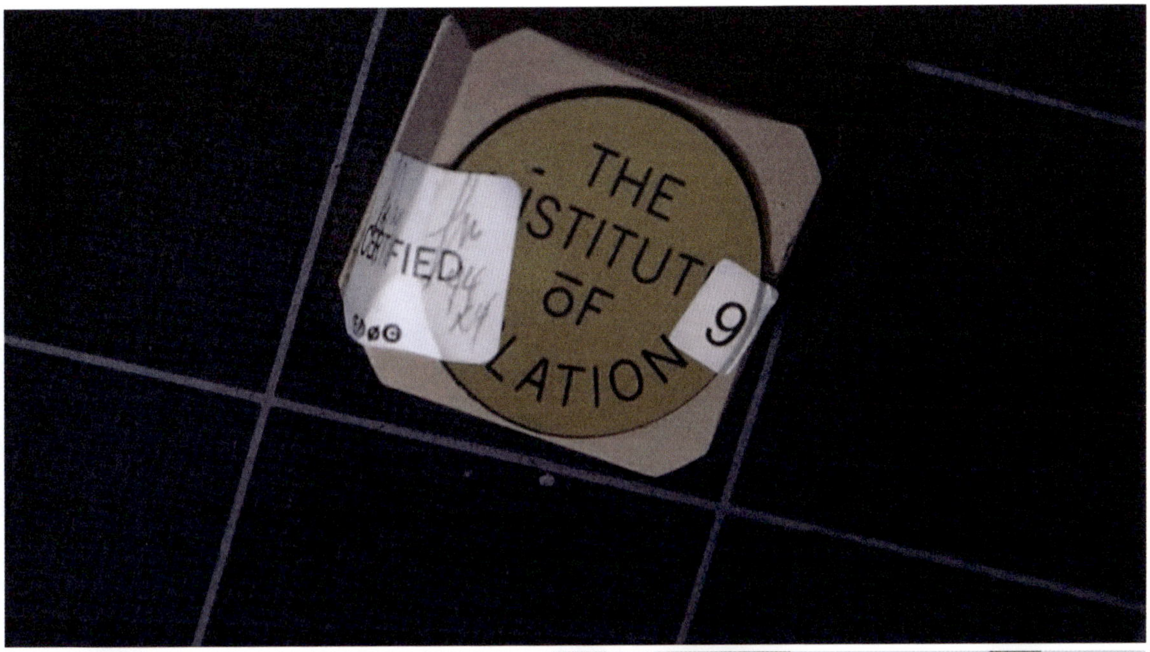

3

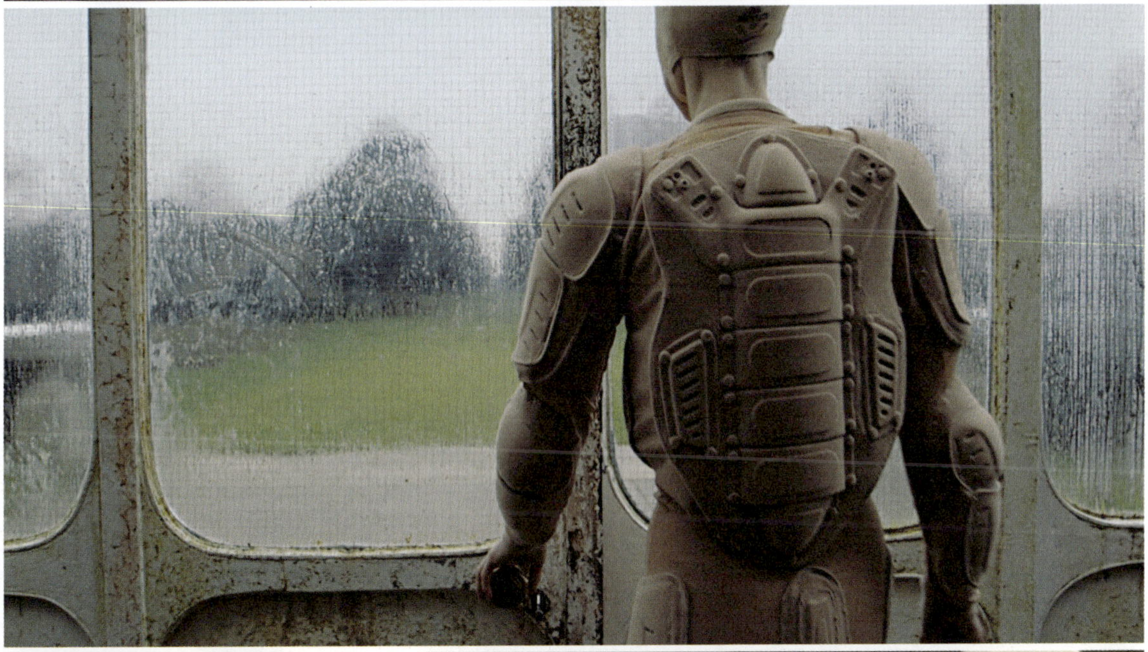

4

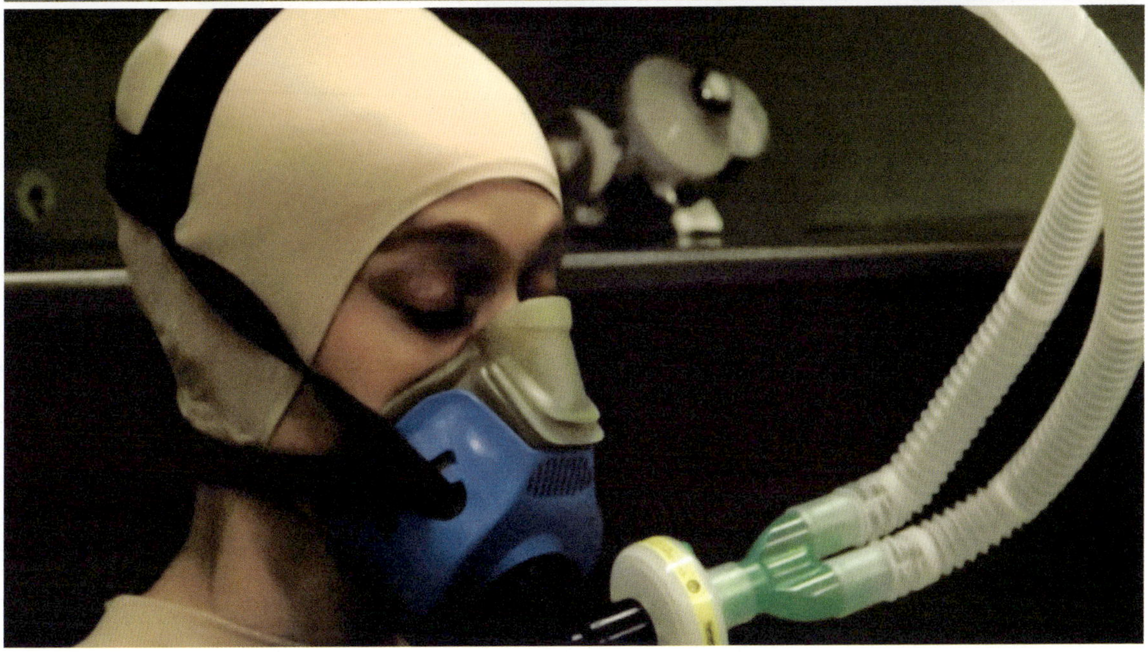

5

The Great Animal Orchestra, Bernie Krause and United Visual Artists
2016–19

Can space be expressed through sound? Bioacoustician and scientist Bernie Krause has documented environments all over the world in forensic detail by recording thousands of wildlife habitats, including oceans and rainforests. Krause proposes that by listening, we can learn an immense amount about the social and geographic components of a given space, as well as the overall health of its inhabitants. Lacking the terminology to describe these distinct acoustic components, Krause invented his own: geophony encompasses all nonbiological sounds, such as water rushing over rocks; biophony is the collective sound made by all the animal species in a given habitat; and anthrophony is the term for human-made sound. *The Great Animal Orchestra* installation is a spectacular immersive experience that presents five thousand hours of Krause's sound recordings of more than fifteen thousand individual species. Taking segments of audio from habitats in the Amazon rain forest and sites across Africa and North America, the installation manifests sounds as spectrograms. Collaborating with Krause in creating the installation, London–based United Visual Artists conceived the vibrating colors that stream across huge screens. Embedded in and reflected by a small pool of water, these are not video images; rather, a computer program processes the recordings in real time, giving the data visual form.

1. Installation view of *The Great Animal Orchestra* at the Fondation Cartier pour l'art contemporain in Paris, 2016.
2. The spectrograms formed an abstract landscape in changing colors that enveloped the audience.
3. Bernie Krause's recordings were rendered in 3-D by United Visual Artists, suggesting scenes from the natural world.

2

3

157

breakthroug

Over the last century or so, the role of the architect has not typically extended to the physical act of building. The breakthrough projects included in this chapter, however, demonstrate how a new generation of practitioners is putting the process of making and construction at the heart of their work—from experimenting with found materials to testing the limits of bricks, bamboo, and marble, and even growing their own hemp to be used in prefabricated panels for cladding. The lateral-thinking and pluralistic practices of the architects featured here seek to reshape the future of the discipline. Several fascinating architectural renewal projects in this chapter share principles of consensus seeking and designing of not only buildings, but also economic drivers and ecosystems as forms of regeneration. In Liverpool, a studio collaborated with an existing grassroots campaign to preserve a number of Victorian houses and a community of working-class streets, mostly abandoned after government disinvestment. In Chicago, agricultural, arts, and educational initiatives invest in destitute city blocks. Halfway around the world, architects collaborated with village elders from a rural province in China on a sequence of acupunctural transformations that range from instituting systems that can support e-commerce to founding new cultural museums and factories that utilize skills and materials of the region. These collaborative and hybrid offices, many founded by women, offer an optimistic view of the future where architects are hired to work in tandem with their environment, reconnecting with the often messy matter of accretion, in whatever form it may take.

Hikma Religious and Secular Complex,
Atelier Masōmī and Studio Chahar
Dandaji, Niger, 2018

1

2

As part of her studies in architecture, Mariam Kamara examined the pre- and postcolonial architectural history of her native Niger, a country in northwestern Africa. She sees designing civic space as an opportunity to be a conduit for meaningful change. Her studio, Atelier Masōmī, is a champion of upholding the earthen architecture traditions of the region, reducing or eliminating imported synthetic or Western-standard building materials,[6] and training and employing local craftspeople. This mosque and community center in the western Niger village of Dandaji uses only three materials, all taken from a 3 mi. (5 km) radius of the site: recycled metal, compressed earth bricks of local laterite soil, and cement. The brief was initially to tear down a dilapidated adobe mosque on the site, built in the 1980s, but Kamara — in collaboration with Yasaman Esmaili of Tehran- and Boston-based Studio Chahar — lobbied to restore it, citing its architectural significance. After consulting with members of the community the architects were made cognizant of the lack of educational organizations for women in the area, so it was decided that the mosque should become a new learning center, which children and women from nearby villages could attend. Renovating the old mosque was an opportunity for the masons of the original building to share their knowledge of traditional masonry, while for the new mosque on the adjacent plot, the architects shared modernized techniques in exchange.

1 The new mosque was built with compressed-earth brick, a material with similar thermal advantages as the adobe brick used in the old mosque.
2 The two buildings form a campus with an outdoor prayer space suitable for celebrations.
3 The new mosque, which is formed primarily from two blocks and a minaret.

Breakthroughs

Hikma Religious and Secular Complex, Atelier Masōmī and Studio Chahar
Dandaji, Niger, 2018

4   Recesses between pillars of the old mosque now house bookshelves.
5   The once derelict mosque is home to a library and community center, encouraging literacy among young adults in the region.
6   The project is a culture and education hub where the secular and religious peacefully coexist.

Breakthroughs

163

A Songyang Story, Xu Tiantian
Songyang, China, 2014–20

DnA_Design and Architecture, a Beijing-based studio lead by Xu Tiantian, invested years of strategic thinking in a complex and multifaceted regeneration project in the picturesque county of Songyang in the Zhejiang province of southeastern China, resulting in a rural renaissance. Many of the smaller villages in this region had fallen into disrepair as young people migrated to urban centers. With the introduction of high-speed national railway links and broadband internet access in the county already set in motion by the Chinese government, the architecture team collaborated with the local and provincial government and community leaders to find economic and cultural forms of stimulus through architecture. Xu and her team launched multiple building and social projects. The studio designed a local history and culture museum; a village hall; a tea house; an inhabited bridge; new factories for the production of rice wine, brown sugar, and tofu; and many formal and informal arts spaces. One village saw a 500 percent increase in tourists per month after the 2015 opening of the museum. The architecture projects' construction involved regional masons and local materials. The team worked closely with stakeholders including politicians and community groups to find ways to lift the spirits and improve the economic status of the people living in these communities, with one project encouraging villagers to use generations-old handicrafts techniques to produce crafts to sell online.

1   Aerial view of the rice wine factory in Shantou village.
2   The tofu factory in Caizhai village, which enables family run workshops to meet production standards suitable to allow the sale of their goods in supermarkets.
3   A view of the spiraling Dushan leisure center, which contains a visitor center, water sports facilities, and a gym, adjacent to the Songyin river.
4   Aerial view of the domed bamboo theater in a forest in Hengkeng village. The theater hosts activities ranging from opera performances to individual meditation.

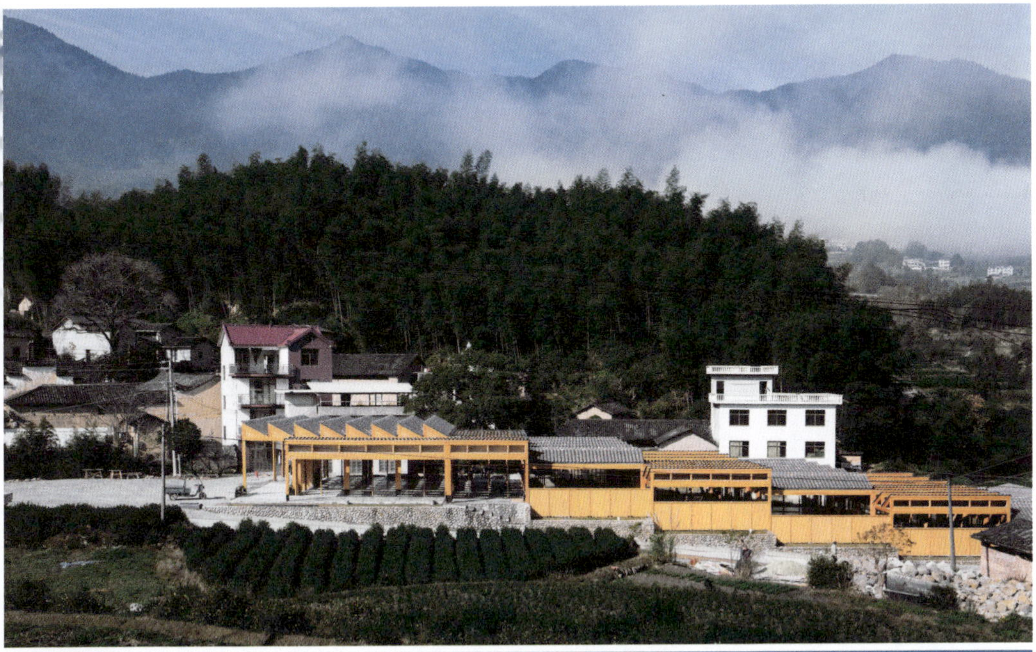
2

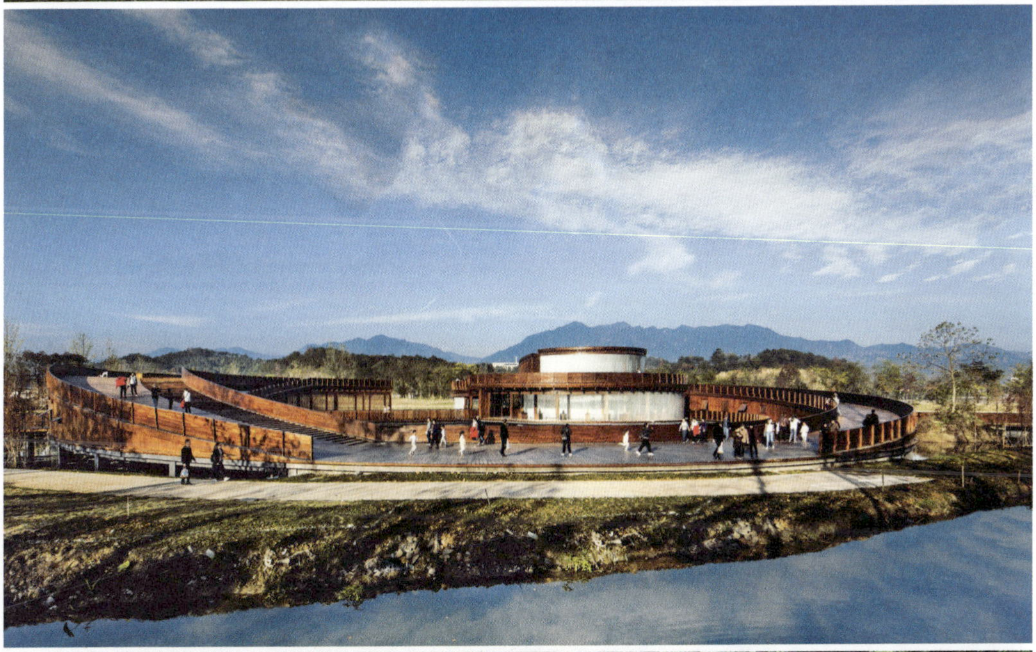
3

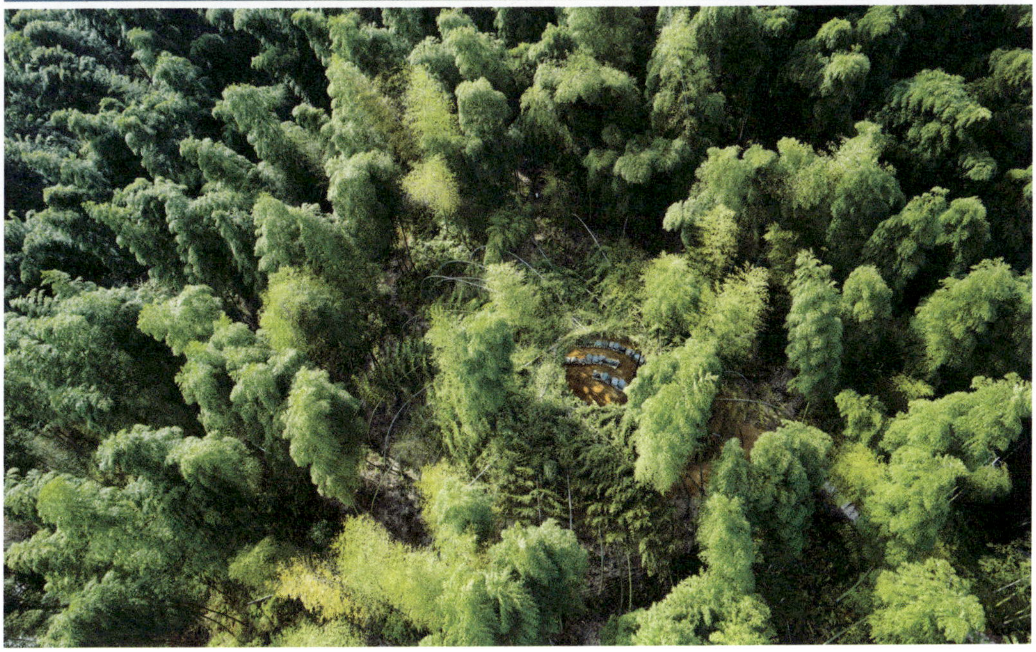
4

A Songyang Story, Xu Tiantian
Songyang, China, 2014–20

5 At work in the tofu factory. The structure functions as a production facility but can also be used by the community to host events.
6 The top floor of the Pingtian village for handicrafts. The wooden structure connects two existing rammed-earth-wall buildings below.
7 The Shimen Bridge links the villages of Shimen and Shimenyu, which were previously separated by the Songyin river.
8 The bridge also hosts markets.

Breakthroughs

Serpentine Pavilion, Frida Escobedo
London, England, UK, 2018

Each summer a pavilion is erected in the forecourt of the Serpentine Galleries in Kensington Gardens, designed by a prominent name in international architecture. Mexico City–based Frida Escobedo was the youngest architect, aged thirty-eight, to receive the prestigious commission. The pavilion is temporary; at the end of summer, the work is sold to a collector and moved to a new location. Escobedo thought about this permanence and lack of site specificity as an intriguing contradiction to the limited nature of the original brief. With this in mind and the prime meridian in Greenwich just a few miles away, the architect decided to use time as an organizing principle. The design consists of two shifted volumes, which surround an enclosed courtyard, aligning on one side with the north–south axis, and on the other, the summer solstice aligns the ceiling's shadow with a shallow pool. The other walls of the angled volumes line up with the Serpentine Gallery in front, creating a Russian doll of interiority and exteriority where the park and the walls create spaces within spaces. The material of the pavilion itself is sourced entirely locally: gray brick roof tiles are stacked and repeated at slightly different angles to mimic *celosías*, a type of permeable wall common in Mexico, and which Escobedo uses as a signature in her work. The design introduces visitors to ways of perceiving space and time, rather than only measuring it.

1   The latticed structure creates an internal courtyard at the center of the pavilion.
2   The pavilion's porous surface seemingly shifts from opaque to transparent as a visitor moves through the space.
3   Exterior view of the pavilion, with the slate roof of the Serpentine Gallery in the background.

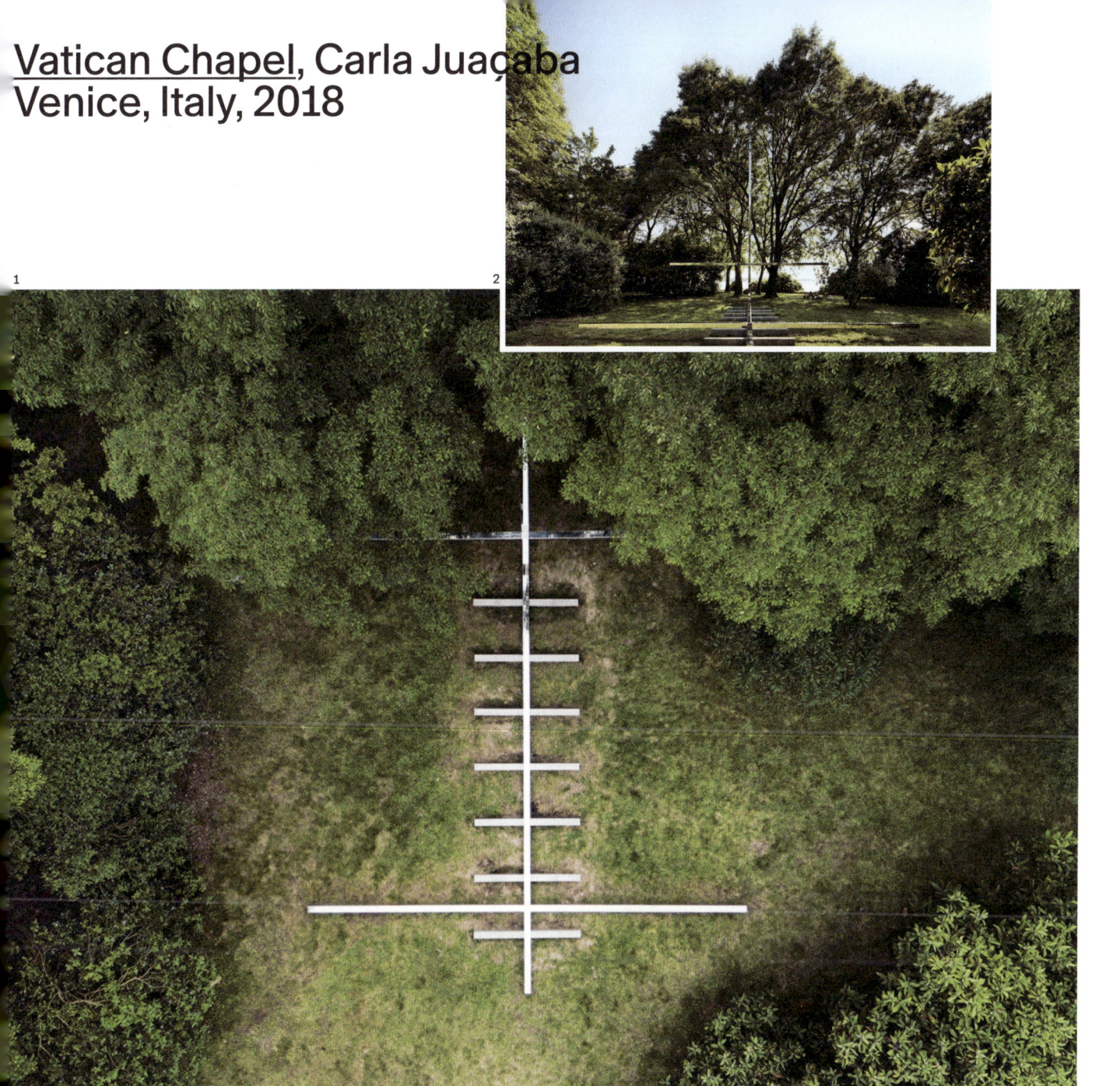

Vatican Chapel, Carla Juaçaba
Venice, Italy, 2018

Rio de Janeiro–based Carla Juaçaba was one of ten contemporary architects invited to design a temporary chapel amid a wooded site on the small island of San Giorgio Maggiore as part of a larger commission for Vatican City's first presence at the 2018 International Architecture Exhibition of the Venice Biennale. Like much of her work, Juaçaba's proposal is beautifully simple. The chapel has no roof or walls but is scored, like musical notes, through small but strategically chosen placements of elements in space — the surrounding trees form a dome, and the movement of people as well as the ritualistic nature of prayer take the place of walls to enclose the chapel. The structure comprises four mirror-polished stainless-steel beams that together make two crosses: one upright, the other on the grassy ground. The entire structure rests on seven pieces of concrete. Depending on the reflections of the sun and trees in the chapel's mirrored edges, at certain times of day it seems to disappear. The creation of space that is not permanent and demarcated by walls references other serene chapels, such as Tadao Ando's 1999 Church of the Light in Ibaraki, Japan — there, Ando uses light, rather than material, to form a cross. In this project, Juaçaba's intent is for the chapel to provide a sacred space around anyone who sits on the beams.

1 Seen from a bird's-eye view, the plan of the chapel takes a form common to churches since the Middle Ages: a cross.
2 In elevation, looking toward the Venetian Lagoon, the pavilion seemingly disappears as the surrounding trees reflect in its surface.

Z33 new wing, Francesca Torzo
Hasselt, Belgium, 2019

In the small medieval Belgian city of Hasselt, the cultural institution Z33: House for Contemporary Art, Design, and Architecture has earned an outsize reputation for its cutting-edge art and design exhibitions. When it needed a new wing, the institution commissioned the young architect Francesca Torzo — based in Genoa, Italy — who trained with Swiss master architect Peter Zumthor, to design it. For this project, Torzo established a manifesto of sorts for a quiet, aleatory way of designing spaces that are expected to be touched; architecture that speaks to history but will grow and transform over time. After studying the many varieties and forms of bricks used to produce much of the fifteenth- and sixteenth-century civic architecture in the region, Torzo developed her ideas for a palette of hues and brick-making ideas for the exterior wall — a solid curtain of triangular bricks of 103 individual types, each precisely drawn and modeled in advance, with each shadow and texture carefully considered. The new wing is an ensemble of simple rooms that vary in size, proportion, illumination, and atmosphere and that overlook each other: the complexity of the spatial pattern echoes that of a city, with gradients between public and private, exposed and intimate.

1   1:10 scale model of the entrance to the Z33 new wing. The model shows where the extension meets the historical building; the new facade harmonizes with the brick architecture of the existing context.
2   A total of 34,494 handmade bricks were placed one by one on the 197-ft.-long (60 m) and 39-ft.-high (12 m) facade.

2

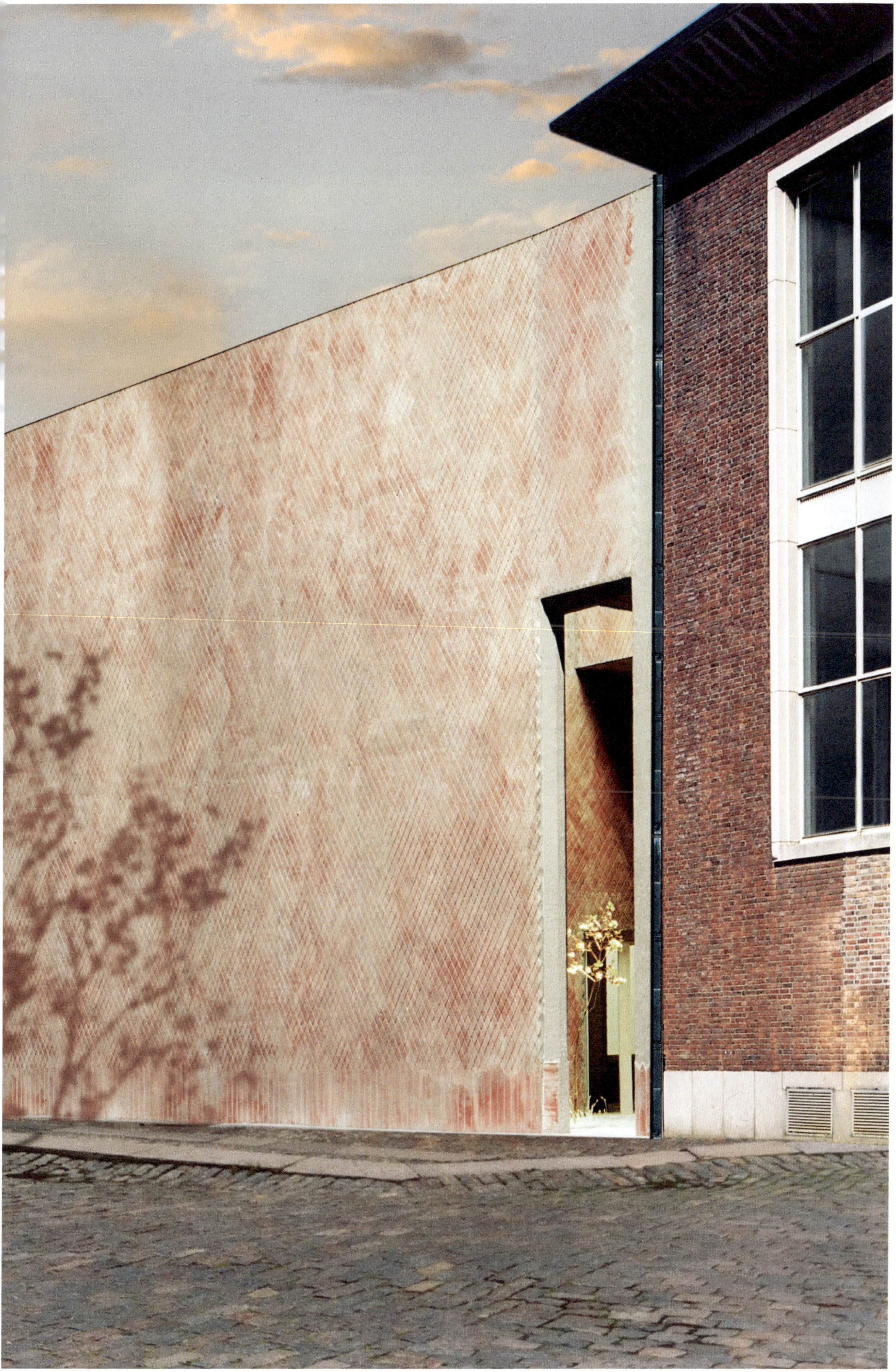

Z33 new wing, Francesca Torzo
Hasselt, Belgium, 2019

5

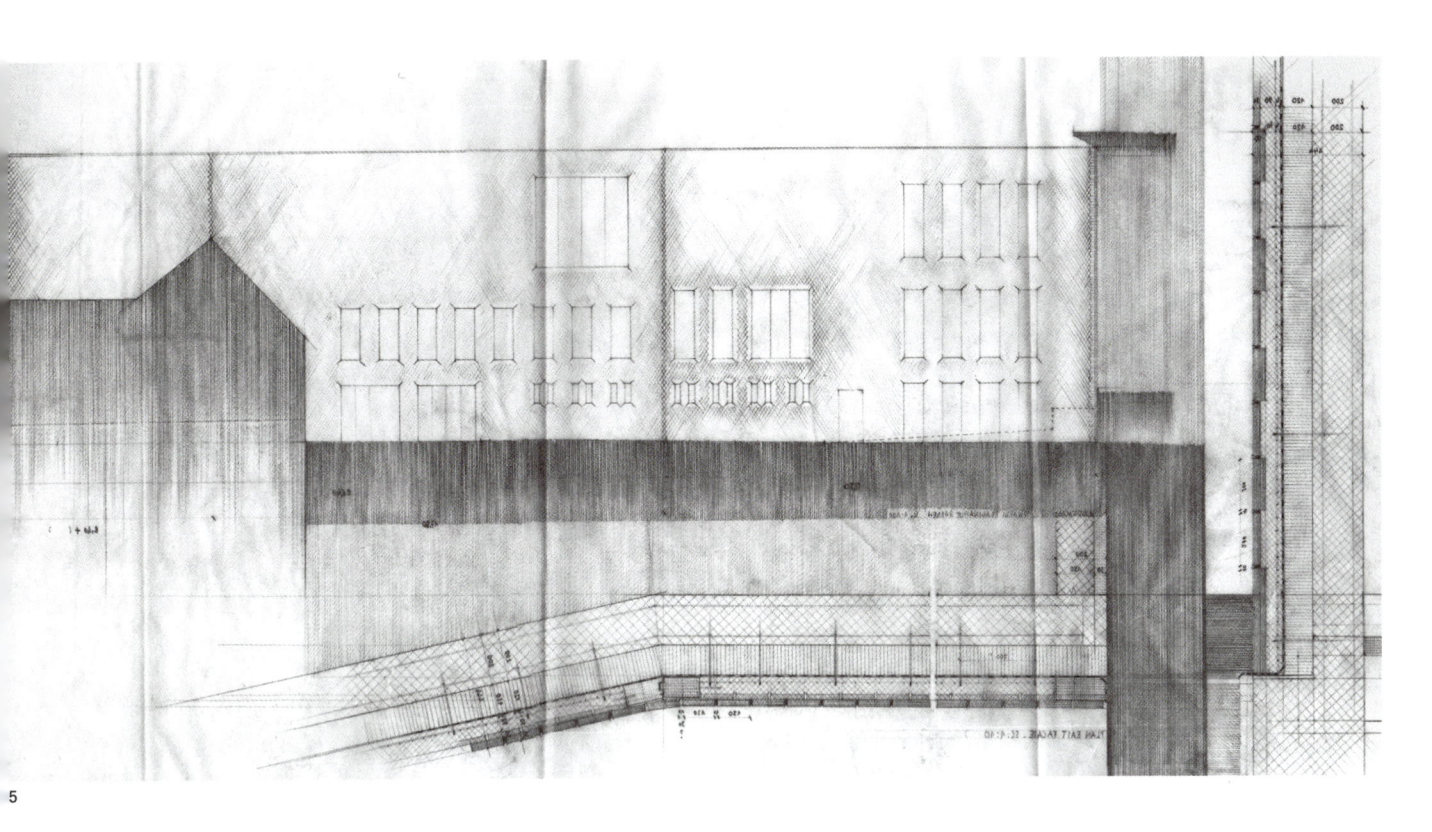

3 The entrance vestibule.
4 1:10 scale model representing a portion of the new wing's interior, an ensemble of simple rooms that shift in size, tone, and proportion.
5 Elevation drawing.
6 One of the exhibition spaces.

Breakthroughs 173

L'air pour l'air, SO—IL
Chicago, IL, USA, 2017

Frequently found in exhibitions, impermanent architecture offers a short-term, typically very low-cost way for young studios to test ideas and make an impact on an often global audience. In this commission for the second Chicago Architecture Biennial in 2017, SO—IL, a New York–based architecture studio, explored the ways in which the exterior material of architecture — its skin — can be used in experimental forms and operate in tandem with its environment in a playful and thoughtful way. For the performance, created in collaboration with artist Ana Prvački and set in the Garfield Park Conservatory, the architects tested architectural forms and geometries at a human scale. An ensemble of four musicians wore custom-made mesh fabric suits, designed to purify the air for the artists as they gave an unearthly performance of composer Veronika Krausas' *De Aere* (concerning the air) quartet. As the performers moved through space, the audience watched as they conjured images of the alienating extremities of our search for purity, privacy, and survival. Through this, the architects sought to question the relationship between body, self, and the environment we breathe through the intimacy of the home, offering the potential for the skin itself to change with different conditions and to radically question individual tolerances and capacity for physical and emotional transparency.

1 Close-up installation and performance view.
2 The suits were worn by an ensemble of saxophone, flute, trombone, and vocals from the Chicago Sinfonietta.
3 The work was inspired by the abundant plant life in the Garfield Park Conservatory in Chicago.

Breakthroughs 175

Granby Four Streets, Assemble
Liverpool, England, UK, 2013–

London-based Assemble is among the most exciting and pluralistic studios working today. Its sixteen members, most of whom studied architecture at Cambridge University, hold expertise in fields spanning history, literature, art, and philosophy to architecture and planning. Their work focuses on intelligent regeneration, often collaborating with grassroots community groups, local governments, arts organizations, and universities to create nonhierarchical social spaces. For this project in Granby, a neighborhood in the port city of Liverpool, the designers joined forces with a community campaign that was fighting for the preservation of four streets of derelict Victorian terraced houses that the local government had marked for demolition. The community association and many other groups had spent years fighting the council's decision, planting vegetables and flowers, and fruit trees in the streets of shuttered-up homes. Assemble worked with Granby Four Streets Community Land Trust and investment group Steinbeck Studios on a long-term vision to secure funding, restore the abandoned homes, and make them available on the market. The consortium also sought to improve the social space of the streets. One home, deemed unsuitable for living, was transformed into the Granby Winter Garden, a community space where locals can hold meetings, socialize, and take part in craft workshops. Assemble was awarded the Turner Prize for its role in the project.

1. Public workshops — called the Granby Workshops — enable members of the local community to participate in the regeneration process by casting tiles and building furniture for use in the homes.
2. A model of one of the homes.
3. One of the derelict Victorian terraced houses that the local government had marked for demolition.

Chapel in Guastalla, Go Hasegawa
Guastalla, Italy, 2017

This serene all-marble chapel in the small town of Guastalla, in northern Italy, is a study in material and light by Japanese architect Go Hasegawa. The mayor of Guastalla invited him to build a contemporary public monument and mourning space for the city's largely Renaissance-era cemetery. Two extremely large pieces of five-hundred-million-year-old Estremoz marble were used to construct the project. Stone is rarely used in construction in Japan, in part due to the country's vulnerability to earthquakes, so the commission was Hasegawa's first encounter with the material. The project's intimate, elegant form responds to three historic references in European architecture: the ancient cave in Matera, Italy; a window niche and bench in a castle in the French commune of Treigny-Perreuse-Sainte-Colombe; and the *nicchia facciata*, a half-domed niche in the facade of a Renaissance building in which a sculpture is placed. In their Tokyo–based studio, Hasegawa's team used blocks of polystyrene to test shaving and sculpting methods by hand. Consequently, the marble was divided into thirteen pieces, with each piece changing in its profile from a thickness of 15 in. (38 cm) at the top and bottom to a thickness of 0.4 in. (1 cm) in the niche at its center. In Hasegawa's inverted *nicchia facciata* — the niche being in the interior, not the exterior — the stone becomes almost translucent. Without a roof, the chapel is open to the sky.

1 The interior of the chapel is open to the sky, furnished only by a simple black plinth.
2 At middle points, the marble walls become so thin they are translucent, appearing to glow in parts.

Flat House, Practice Architecture
Cambridgeshire, England, UK, 2019

London-based studio Practice Architecture creates long-lasting and scalable low-carbon buildings, and finds their novel architectural language through an innovative use of natural and low-carbon materials. This project was commissioned by Margent Farm, with whom the studio also developed the building's unusual cladding. The farm grows industrial hemp, a fast-growing strain of the cannabis plant that sequesters large amounts of carbon as it grows. For centuries it has been used in ropes and textiles, but it is also a viable alternative to the ecologically harmful plastics that are often used in practice construction arduistry. The Flat House, a three-bedroom prototype, was assembled using prefabricated panels infilled with insulation made of the farm's processed hemp shiv, mixed with lime and water. The cladding is composed of the hemp fiber soaked with a sugar-based resin derived from agricultural waste then pressed into sheets. In addition to the very low levels of embodied carbon used to construct the building, the home is mostly "off-grid," meaning that it generates its heat and electrical power using a biomass boiler and photovoltaic roof panels, only relying on the local infrastructure for its water supply. Public interest in the project led to the formation of Material Cultures, a sister research organization, which is exploring how hundreds of hemp houses could be mass-produced using off-site construction systems across the United Kingdom.

1   Exterior view of the Flat House, showing the hemp fiber and bio-resin cladding developed for the project. The new building takes the footprint of an existing barn.
2   Interior view of the house showing the prefabricated hemp panels.
3   A double-height yet intimate living space inside the Flat House.

Breakthroughs

Taobao Village — Smallacre City, Drawing Architecture Studio, 2018

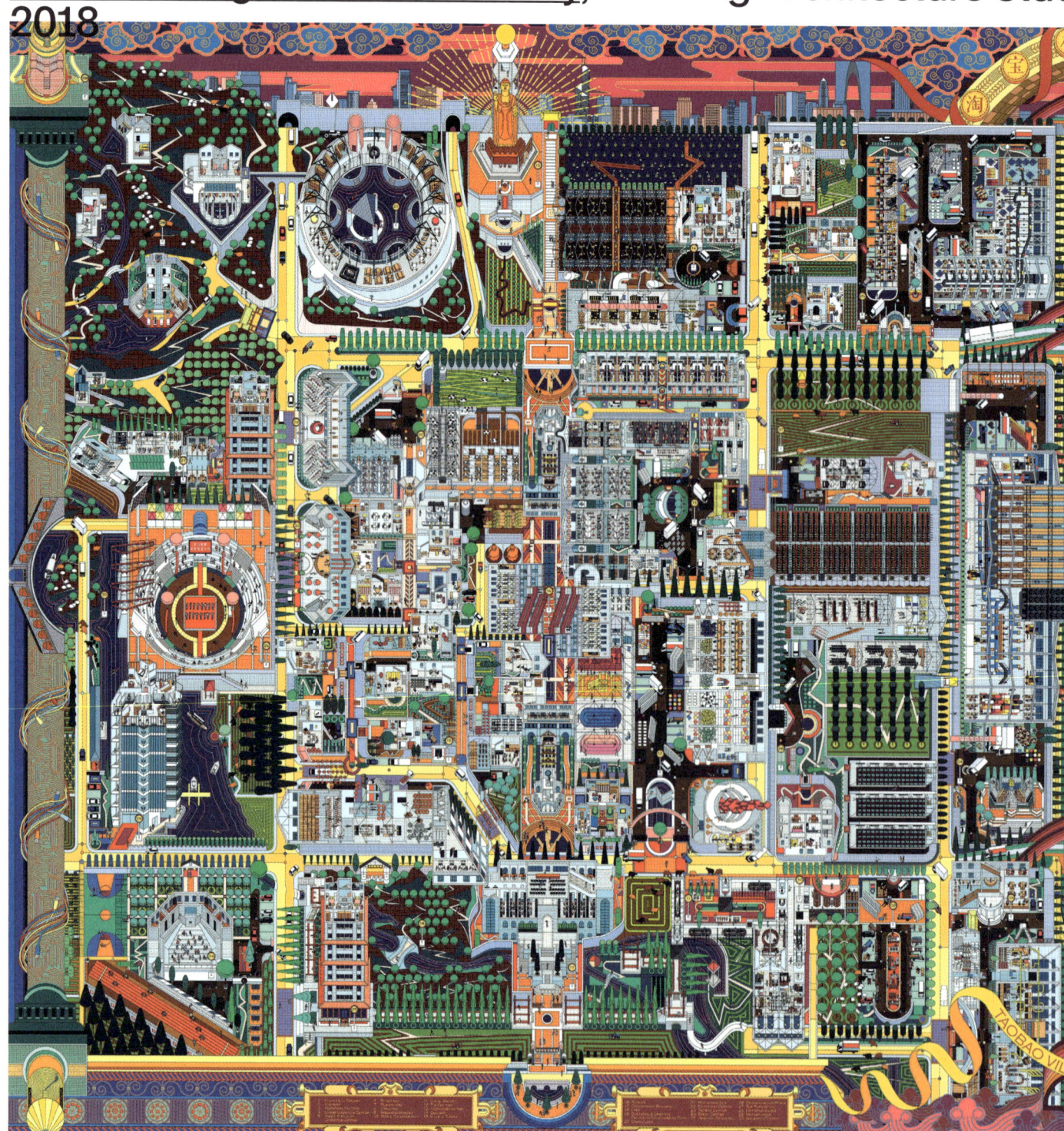

The history of architecture is peppered with grand proposals for urban utopias. Ivan Leonidov's proposal for the new city Magnitogorsk, Kisho Kurokawa's Agricultural City, Archizoom's No-Stop City, and Frank Lloyd Wright's Broadacre City are all unrealized designs that were large-scale, radical, and subversive. Beijing-based Drawing Architecture Studio's large panorama Taobao Village — Smallacre City playfully and intricately reinterprets Wright's Broadacre City, a polemical decentralized suburban utopia where families had a small parcel of land in which to grow food and build their homes, never depending on government or charity. DAS's joyful, rich, chaotic, and playful imaginary village portrays rural life as powered by Taobao, one of China's biggest online shopping platforms, for which people make anything from pillowcases to medical supplies and sell and distribute directly, consumer to consumer. The village would host the millions of people who make and sell items from their homes, making Taobao's domestic consumerism a potential transition point for the wealth exchange between rural and urban economies in China. The layered, lively cityscape — with bridges, roads, and conveyor belts crossing over and intersecting each other — encompasses both the Taobao enterprise and a rural–urban complex. The vivid axonometric and cross-section drawing techniques of DAS are reminiscent of Tibetan *thangkas* and Persian miniatures.

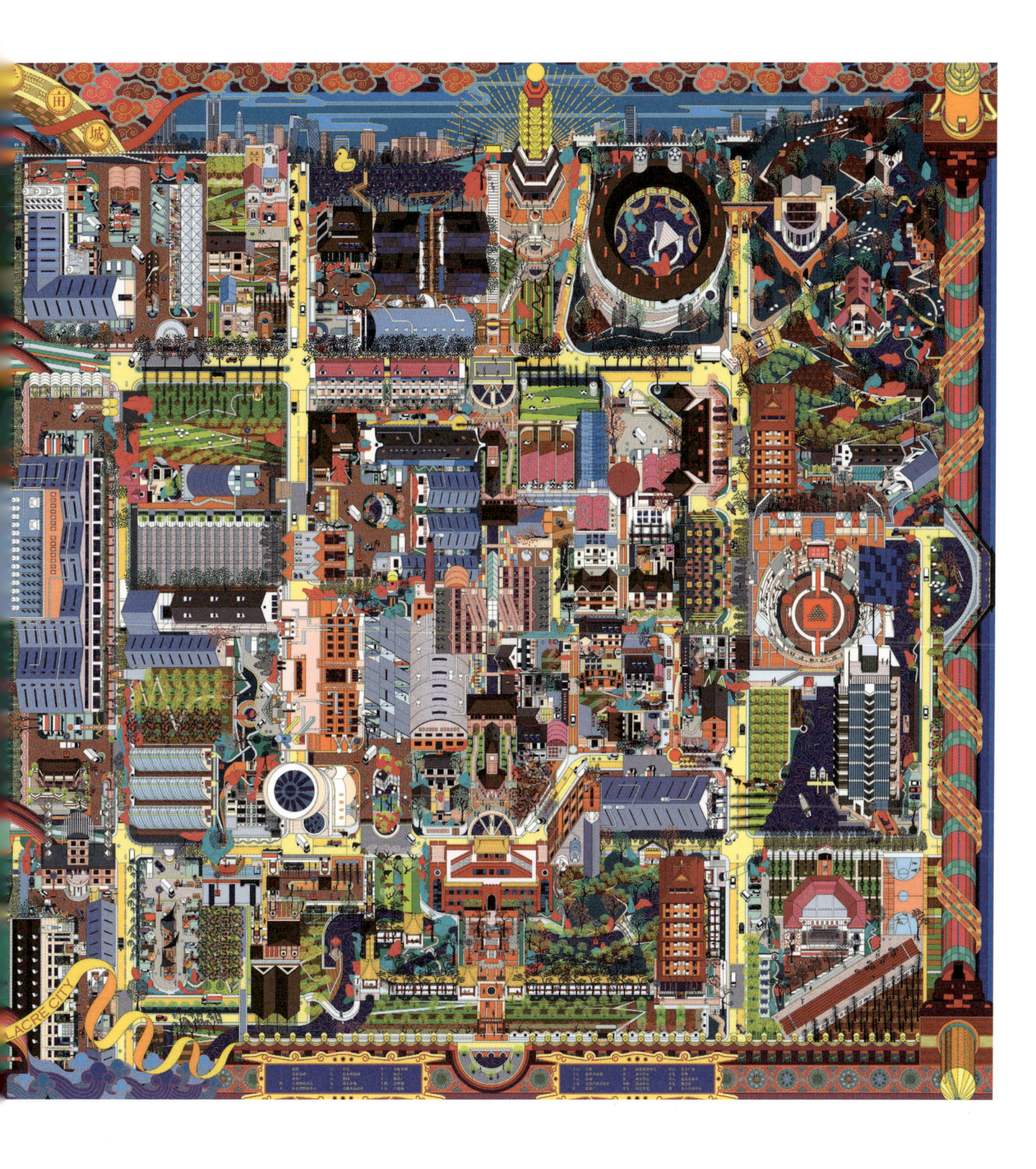

1   A revolution in e-commerce has thrown a lifeline to China's rural producers, who can sell goods via the online marketplace Taobao; the economies of entire villages are now devoted to the platform. While this drawing depicts a virtual village, it is composed of details collected from real "Taobao villages" — clusters of rural e-tailers within an administrative hub.

Structures of Landscape, Ensamble Studio
Fishtail, MT, USA, 2016

Structures of Landscape is a sequence of vast, site-specific constructions commissioned for the 10,000-ac. (4,000 ha) Tippet Rise Art Center, a sheep and cattle ranch just north of Yellowstone National Park in Fishtail, Montana. Each of the sculptural structures had to function as a performance space for classical musicians, but also occupy the environment elegantly. Spanish office Ensamble Studio — whose architecture, art, and teaching practice is rooted in a close dialogue with the earth — examined geological transformation processes, such as sedimentation, erosion, weathering, crystallization, and metamorphism, as a method to repurpose the topography of the remote location. One structure, Domo, houses a series of caverns that were conceived as an upside-down valley. The others, titled Beartooth Portal and Inverted Portal, each consist of two rocklike forms that lean toward each other and touch at their peak. They appear to be in a primordial moment of equilibrium, but, in fact, they are highly engineered. The studio cast each of the three concrete structures from the landscape itself, using huge volumes of soil as formwork and pouring the concrete in situ. After the concrete cured for twenty-eight days, two of the 330-ton (300 tonne) structures were turned upward, retaining the imprint of the terrain from which they were cast, while Domo was cast in place.

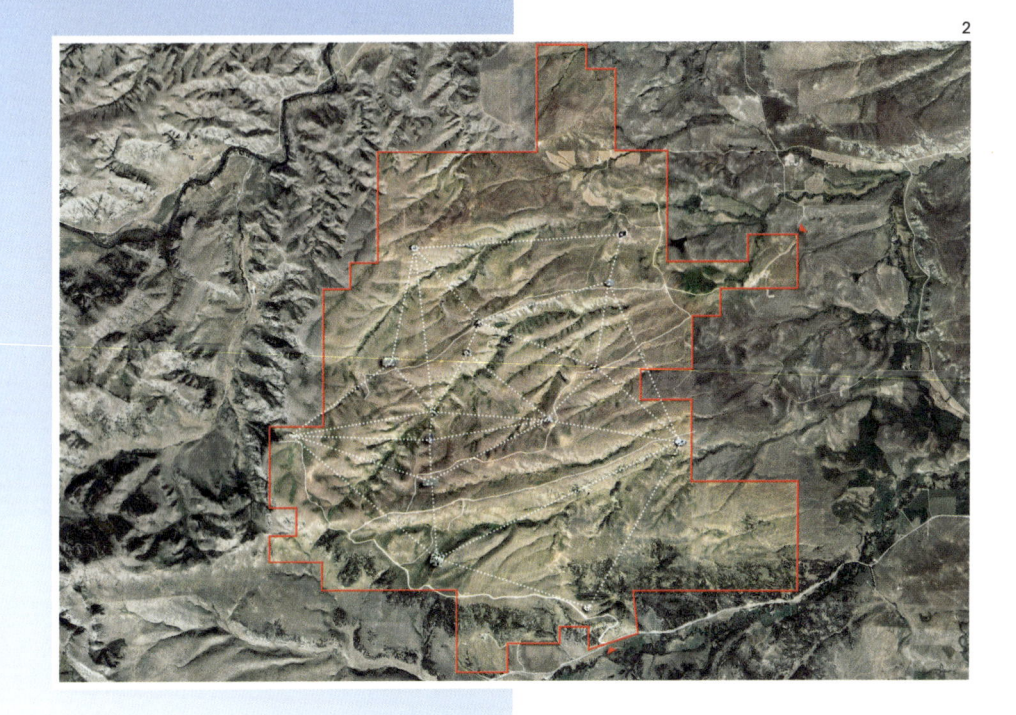

1 Domo, which takes its name from a variation of the Spanish word for "home."
2 The master plan for the Tippet Rise Art Center, which extends over a vast expanse of Montana farmland.

Breakthroughs

Structures of Landscape, Ensamble Studio
Fishtail, MT, USA, 2016

3

3 The two forms of Inverted Portal reflect the upward tectonic plate movement of the Beartooth Mountains beyond.
4 Each earthen structure is made from earth, rock, cement, grass, and reinforcing bar, and bears the imprint of the soil in which it was cast.
5 Beartooth Portal frames views of Murphy Canyon, acting as a continuation of the canyon's inner space.
6 The rolling, expansive landscape of the Tippet Rise Art Center is still a working sheep and cattle farm.

4

184

Breakthroughs 185

Regenerative Neighborhood Development, Sweet Water Foundation
Chicago, IL, USA, 2014–

In the early twentieth century, just after the Great Depression, the United States government initiated a number of strategies to inject wealth into the economy and to support families in buying their own homes. These home loans represented an injection of billions of dollars of wealth for white families. Black families were instead subjected to a mandated policy of segregating and isolation. City planners and banks used red lines on district maps to denote "hazardous" areas that should not receive investment. Banks refused financing for mortgages, home improvements, and student loans to anyone living in these demarcated neighborhoods until 1968, ruling out social mobility through homeownership and reinforcing already systemic poverty endured by people of color. The racist policy, now known as *redlining*, is at the root of the urban decay found in parts of many US cities and is a starting point for the Sweet Water Foundation, founded by Emmanuel Pratt. Together with a team of teachers, artists, and architects, Pratt uses "regenerative neighborhood development" as a mode of practice, seeking to address Chicago's urban blight through cultural investment, and new ways of working with land. SWF took responsibility for four abandoned city blocks in a once-segregated neighborhood in South Chicago and transformed them through farming, the initiation of intergenerational workshops, and conducting educational outreach.

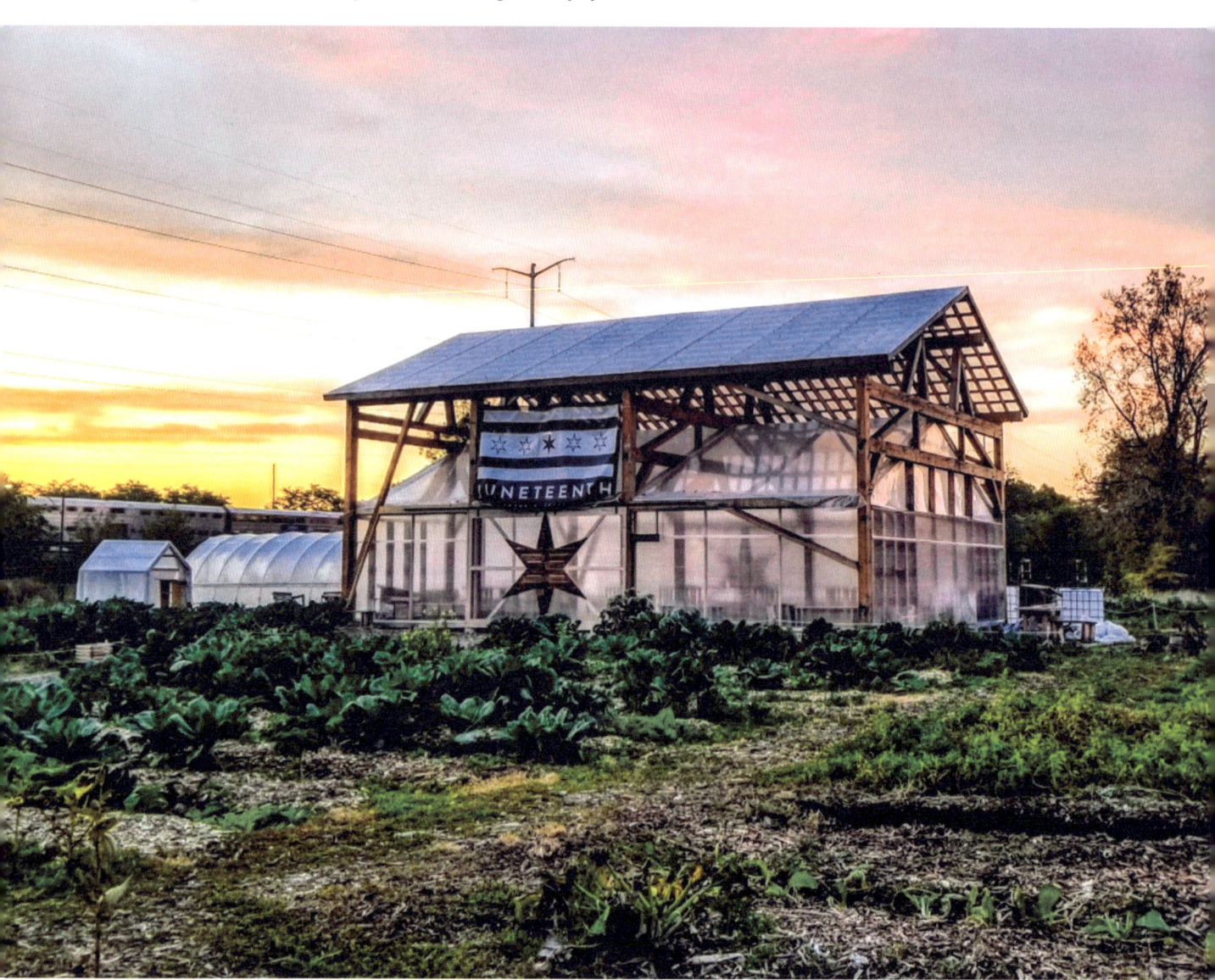

1

1 The hand-raised Thought Barn forms part of the Community Farm in Englewood, Chicago. Sweet Water Foundation reclaims vacant spaces to grow its own produce.
2 An SWF carpentry workshop underway in the greenhouse, with the Think-Do House in the background. Other workshops include beekeeping, yogurt making, canning, and local historic preservation.
3 On the Community Farm, art performances are hosted in the Thought Barn.
4 A "Seeding the Future" school fieldtrip and lunch in the Thought Barn.

2

3

4

187

Bamboo Hostels, Anna Heringer
Baoxi, China, 2016

1

Anna Heringer — an honorary chair of UNESCO's Earthen Architecture, Building Cultures, and Sustainable Development program — looks for ways to build that counterbalance the ecologically damaging twenty-first-century modes of using prefabricated concrete and steel. Her practice seeks to demonstrate the positive economic and social impact of projects that involve local skills, regional materials, and fair working conditions in rural regions and developing countries. In the three years between 2011 and 2014, China consumed more cement than the United States had in the previous century,[7] radically transforming the physical, economic, and cultural landscape of the country. Entire cities popped up filled with mostly concrete apartment buildings and office towers. In a project devoted to reviving traditional ways of building in China, the first International Bamboo Architecture Biennale was launched in the southern region of Baoxi. The curators invited Heringer and her team to design a pilot project to show how this flexible and plentiful material could be used. Heringer and her team created three hostels using undulating, basketlike woven exterior shapes that are inspired by the forms of ceramic vessels that the region is famous for.

1 The Bamboo Hostels project was commissioned as part of the inaugural International Bamboo Architecture Biennale, for which twelve architects were invited to build permanent structures using bamboo.
2 The two hostels and one guesthouse demonstrate the strength of bamboo and utilize the region's rich tradition of craftsmanship, such as basketweaving.

Breakthroughs

Bamboo Hostels, Anna Heringer
Baoxi, China, 2016

3

4

3 Section drawing of the male hostel. Its interior spaces and main circulation routes are predominantly made of rammed earth and stone.
4 Section drawing of the female hostel. Waterproof sleeping cocoons are attached to the central core, visible through the woven bamboo structure.
5 The Bamboo Hostel structures were inspired by the expressive ceramic vessels for which the Baoxi region is famous.
6 The three structures — named the Dragon, the Nightingale, and the Peacock — take different forms but utilize the same materials.

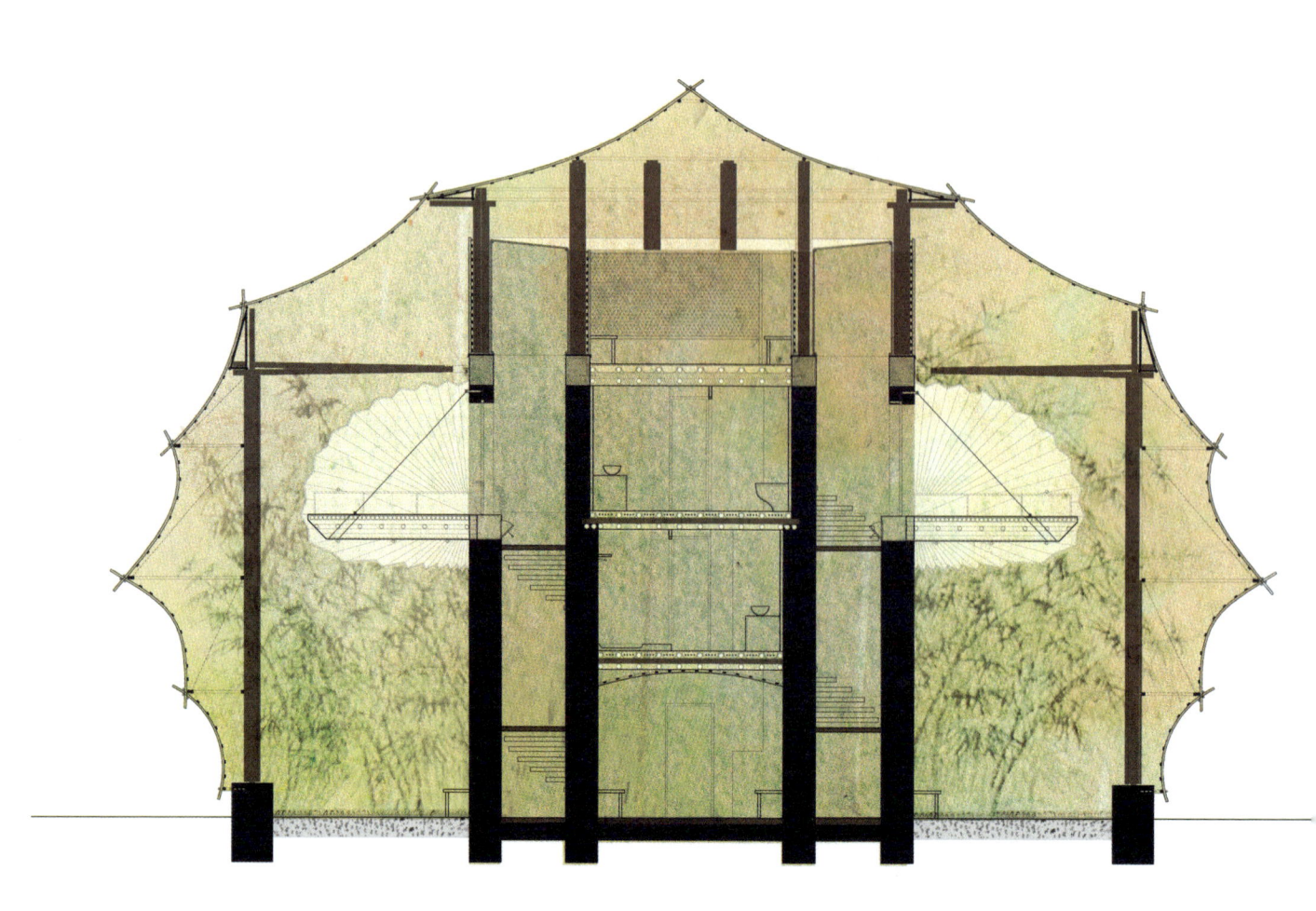

Breakthroughs

Miami Museum Garage, WORKac
Miami, FL, USA, 2018

1

Miami's Design District, a designated area for cultural tourists, is home to many extroverted buildings: flamboyant facades compete for attention on pedestrianized streets. In addition, offices including OMA, Herzog & de Meuron, and TEN Arquitectos have all designed multiuse parking spaces in Miami, flipping the notion of a mundane garage on its head. New York–based architecture studio WORKac was among a number of firms commissioned by curator and architect Terence Riley to conceive different sections of the attention-grabbing exterior of this seven-story parking garage. The firm's playful wnd critical thinking combined to reimagine the potential of the "skin" of a building. For their corner piece of the structure, the architects used the vertical space of the 65.6-ft.-high (20 m), 6.6-ft.-deep (2 m) exterior to build a functioning social space inside the wall of the facade, incorporating a swimming pool, day care center, DJ booth, garden with a single palm tree, lending library, and gallery for graffiti art. Designed as a kind of urban ant farm, the Museum Garage serves as a compendium of WORKac's interests in accessible and self-sustaining design systems: a multipurpose building that operates as a space for experimentation, familiar elements combined in innovative ways to generate unexpected communal activities, and architectural diversity created through the variety of exaggerated forms and colors.

Breakthroughs

2

1 At the roof level, a few parking spaces have been removed to accommodate a small auditorium and beachlike space.
2 WORKac's corner section of the garage facade was conceived without the office knowing what any of the other architecture firms had designed, much like a game of exquisite corpse.

193

Miami Museum Garage, WORKac
Miami, FL, USA, 2018

3

4

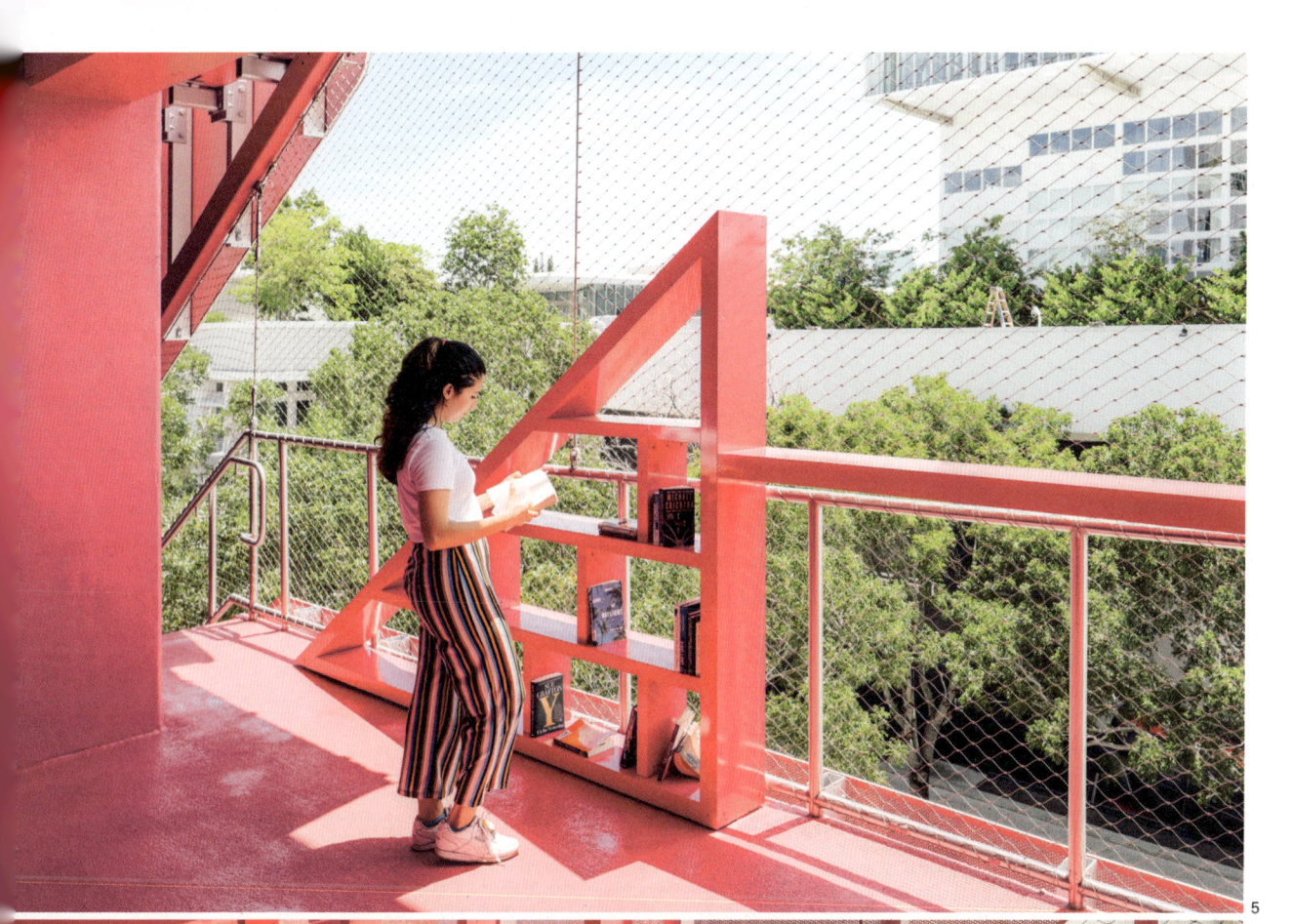

3   The children's play area, which features a slide and climbing wall.
4   Bright pink public zones include space for leisure.
5   A section of the lending library.
6   The meshed-screen facade is punctured with oversized round apertures.

Breakthroughs 195

mastermind

This chapter introduces the philosophers, scientists, filmmakers, artists, curators, and academics rewiring the mainframe of architectural thought. From writing books to building a university curriculum, the work and ideas of this group have profoundly influenced contemporary design theory and discourse. Challenging the status quo and metaphorically and literally interrogating what lies beneath the surface, these masterminds have added new terminologies to the field as well as entirely new attitudes about space and place. A number encourage a renewed reading of the biological intimacy between people and the nonhuman animals in their environments, whether through a video game that is a philosophy lesson, or the story telling of an ecofeminist philosopher. Many of the projects included here highlight the interconnectedness between the current ecological crisis and other issues of global importance including poverty, war, and social justice, all of which are arguably byproducts of a sustained period of growth and accumulation of wealth in Western societies. These masterminds address these inequalities by creating radical new alliances. Often working at major universities, these singular figures have surprising and illuminating attitudes that in turn inspire other thinkers and makers. Here, the institution of academia itself is also analyzed. The expense and time commitment of an elite higher education that is required to practice as an architect, in tandem with low starting salaries and slow career progression, is widely regarded as an obstruction to diversity in the discipline; in response, a free educational model for postgraduate design, based on decentralized systems of teaching, is realized — an example of just one radical new pathway for the masterminds of tomorrow.

New Dark Age, James Bridle
2018

The writings, research, and art practice of Athens–based James Bridle introduce the complex and often sinister architecture of digital technology to the public with searing clarity. A natural enthusiast, Bridle believes networked computers are the greatest human invention since language, but their book *New Dark Age: Technology and the End of the Future* (2018) also makes a case that the more society depends on a handful of people to centralize its information systems, the less likely a healthy democracy is to survive. The "dark age" Bridle describes emerges from a correlation between the surveilling, data-collecting, and data-generating practices driving many industries, and a climate of simplistic, populist postfactual politics. In an era when incredible technologies could generate knowledge to educate and elevate ourselves, Bridle observes that governments are delegating the role of managing that information to private profit-oriented companies. This lack of transparency behind the structures of power causes misinformation and inequality, making people feel doubt, fear, and anger. Much like architecture, technology infrastructure that is not open to scrutiny, critique, and reuse serves only to amplify existing inequities of power.[8] Bridle also observes the carbon-producing megastructures that power our "wireless" and "cloud" technology. By counting the carbon footprint of data processing, they also demonstrate the ecological costs of these practices.

1 Drone shadow installed at the Zeppelin Museum, Friedrichshafen, Germany, 2019, for the exhibition *Game of Drones. Of Unmanned Aerial Vehicles*.
2 Drone shadow installed for the Aichi Triennale in Nagoya, Japan, 2019.
3 Drone shadow installed at Aksioma — Institute for Contemporary Art in Ljubljana, Slovenia, 2015.

Rafiki, Wanuri Kahiu
2018

1

2

Kenyan filmmaker and story teller Wanuri Kahiu is a champion of pan-African stories. Her movies are serene, luscious fantasies that situate Kenyan tales in the cinematic universe of near-future narratives involving artificial intelligence. She details that her mission as a filmmaker is to alter the way African stories are told on-screen. Kahiu uses the term *Afrobubblegum* to describe her practice and the work of many of her peers across the continent. She celebrates cultural production that is not serious, driven by policy or agenda, but futuristic, playful, imaginative, and light. She has written stories of Nairobi pop bands, for example, who travel into space, inhabit distant worlds, and swap gender roles. Her film *Rafiki* (Swahili for "friend") tells the story of two Kenyan women who fall in love, walking and exploring Nairobi together (the production was initially banned in Kenya, where homosexuality is currently punishable with prison time). Her platform is an opportunity to counterbalance an excess of images of African lives permeated by poverty that have played out on-screen throughout recent history. In reflecting on the asymmetric dissemination of continental Africa to the wider world, Kahiu draws on the lyrics of Somali–Canadian hip-hop artist K'Naan, who remixed an African proverb: "Until the lion learns to speak, the tales of hunting will be meek."[9]

1 The film's two young protagonists, Kena and Ziki, played by Samantha Mugatsia and Sheila Munyiva respectively.
2 Still from *Rafiki*. When it premiered in 2018, it was the first Kenyan film to be screened at the Cannes Film Festival.

X-Ray Architecture, Beatriz Colomina
2019

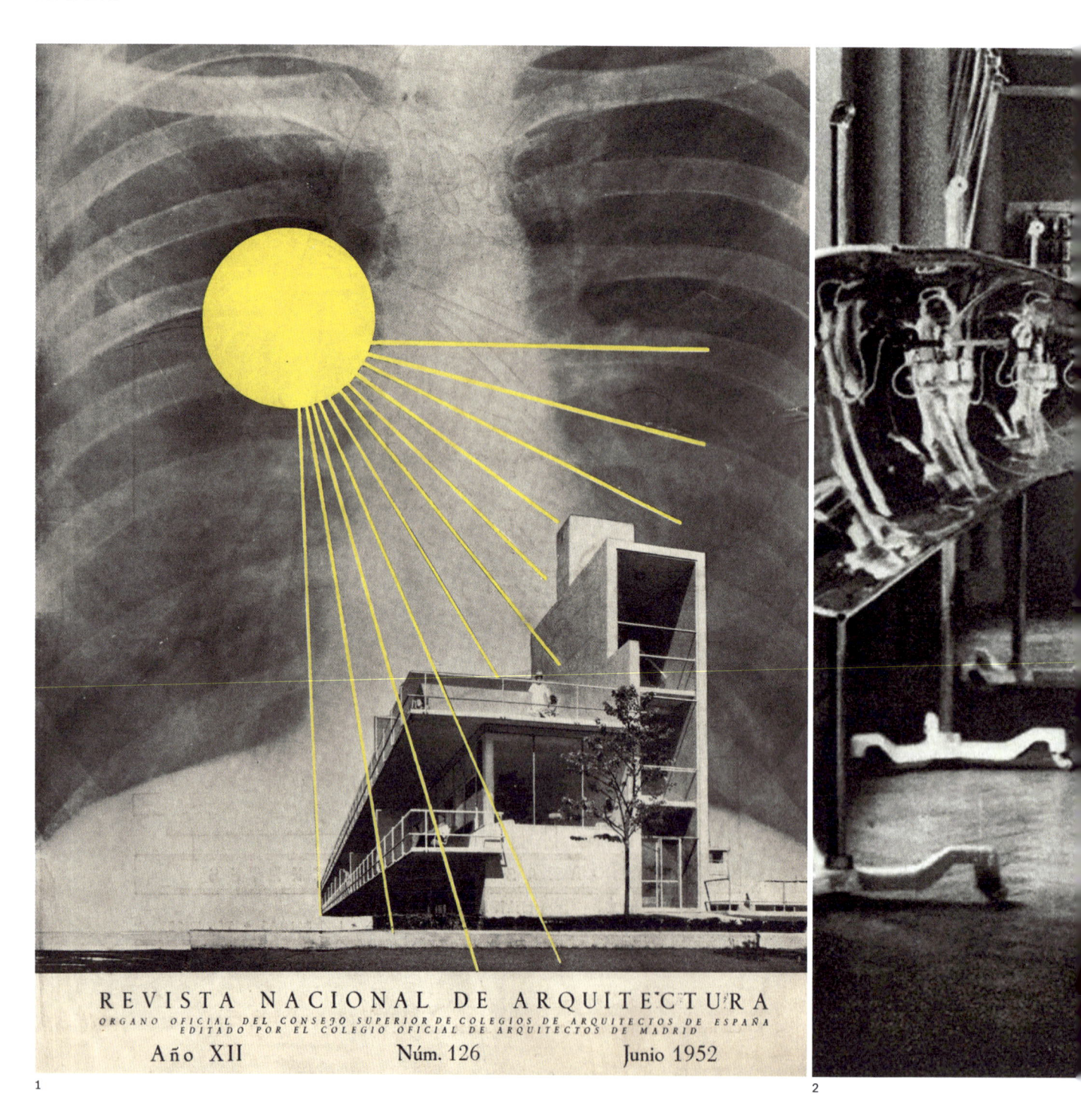

Architectural theorist and Princeton professor Beatriz Colomina's publications and exhibitions examine the history of modernity through lenses such as media, sexuality, and education. Her works express critical ideas about contemporary society. In her book, Colomina draws parallels between the invention and implementation at the turn of the twentieth century of the X-ray — a primary diagnostic tool for tuberculosis — with the dawn and global dissemination of Modern architecture, a movement that espoused ideals of simplicity, light, and cleanliness. In the late nineteenth century, as fear of tuberculosis bpread, curtains and carpets were considered unhygienic and so were replaced by smooth surfaces of ceramics and plastics. Colomina examines the obsession of pioneering Modern architects, such as Le Corbusier and Alvar and Aino Aalto, with illness, and their ideas that their designs could improve health. She asks if the way we see and understand our bodies is also resonant with the way we represent and experience buildings. She notes that Ludwig Mies van der Rohe had a personal collection of X-ray images, this curiosity influencing how he conceived his built work. The new transparency offered by the X-ray scan is considered by Colomina as both an aesthetic and a social tool, allowing the modernity of glass houses and skyscrapers, as well as a radical transformation of privacy.

1 Cover of *Revista Nacional de Arquitectura* 126, June 1952. It shows an image of the Lake County Tuberculosis Sanatorium superimposed on an X-ray of lungs.
2 French children during an indoor helio-therapy session, Paris, 1937.
3 George Keck, Crystal House (1933–34), exhibited at the World's Columbian exhibition in Chicago, 1934. A Dymaxion car by Richard Buckminster Fuller is parked in the garage.

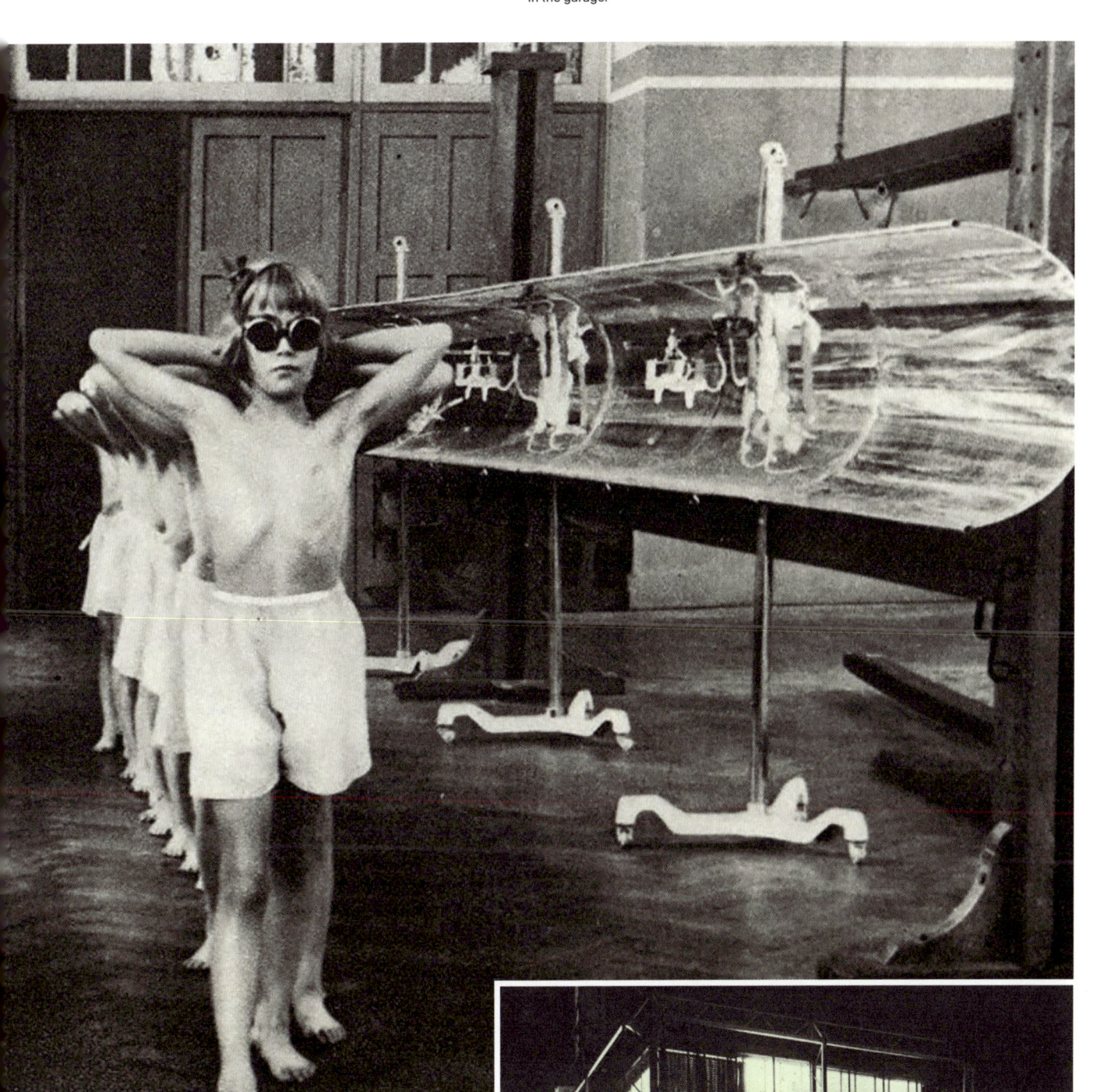

Masterminds

Donna Haraway: Story Telling for Earthly Survival, Fabrizio Terranova 2016

Donna Haraway is a biologist and philosopher who has dedicated her career to researching the relationship between humans and the other organisms with which we share our planet. As an ecofeminist scholar, she has pollinated the way that architects, artists, and urban planners see and design for the world. In her seminal book *Staying with the Trouble: Making Kin in the Chthulucene* (2016), Haraway radically rethinks interspecies relationships, using the term *kin* to describe the deeply interconnected and interdependent life-sustaining ecosystems that exist around humankind. For Haraway, nothing less than a total reconfiguration of our relationship to these systems is needed — she proposes that the cultural commitment humanity reserves for the closest family should be extended to all the animals and plants we live alongside. For architects, this can be seen in a movement toward consciously designing spaces and places for plants and nonhuman animals, appreciating that every gesture of construction is also the making and unmaking of habitats for flora and fauna. A 2016 film dedicated to her ideas, *Donna Haraway: Story Telling for Earthly Survival*, written and directed by Fabrizio Terranova, was responsible for disseminating the Santa Cruz–based philosopher's ideas to a broad public outside of biological and philosophical circles.

1

1 In her seminal 1985 essay "A Cyborg Manifesto," Donna Haraway explored cyborgs from the perspective of feminism, offering the non-gendered beings as a way to understand what it may be to exist as neither male nor female.
2 Director Fabrizio Terranova spent several weeks in conversation with Haraway at her home in Santa Cruz to make the film.
3 The use of green screens allowed ethereal jellyfish and octopi to float by Haraway mid-conversation, the technique capturing her personality as well as her ideas.
4 An intimate portrait, the film explores the feminist theorist's interest in forms of interspecies cooperation or "making kin."

203

Anatomy of an AI System, Kate Crawford and Vladan Joler

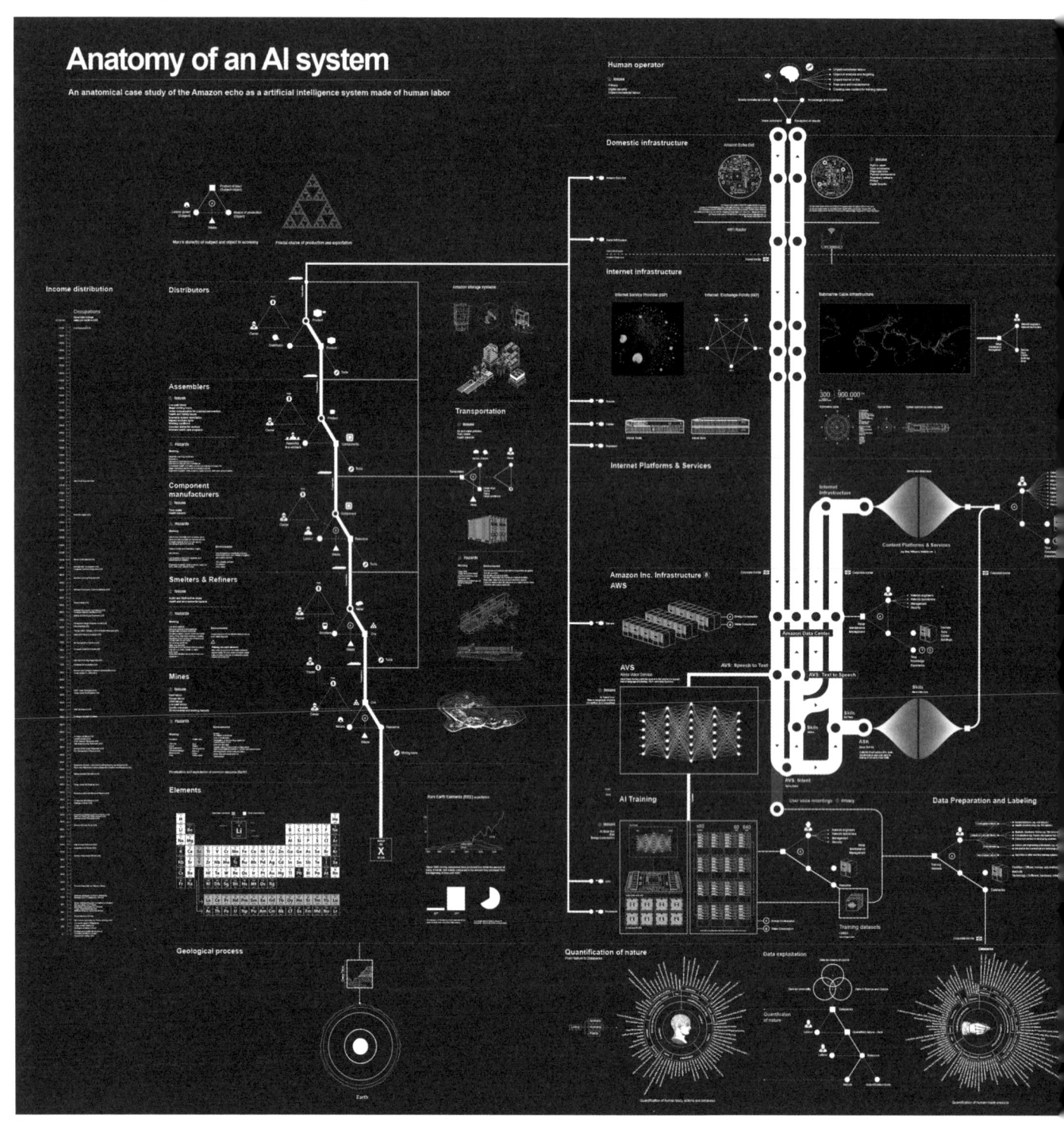

According to French philosopher Bruno Latour, the more comfortable technologies make our lives, the less we feel a need to know how exactly they work. Kate Crawford, co-founder of New York–based AI Now Institute, and Vladan Joler, of the University of Novi Sad, Serbia, were fascinated by the seemingly "magic" capability of Amazon Alexa to listen and respond accurately to voice commands. Their design project Anatomy of an AI System exposes the massive roots system of one of the most complex gadgets on the market today. The work, recently acquired for the New York Museum of Modern Art's permanent collection, is a large-scale map and data visualization project that in simple black-and-white graphics and icons tries to explain for the first time the masses of opaque, interconnected systems of human labor, logistics, data capture, training of artificial intelligence networks, and planetary resources required to build and use a single Amazon Echo (a small, speaker-like device that can receive voice instructions, such as "turn on the radio" or "call Dad"). Crawford and Joler concluded that the elements required to build AI systems are too obscured by intellectual property law and too mired in logistical complexity to fully understand. However, what the work does achieve is to challenge the metaphor of a disembodied "cloud," by exposing the physical realities that underlie our contemporary culture of digital convenience.

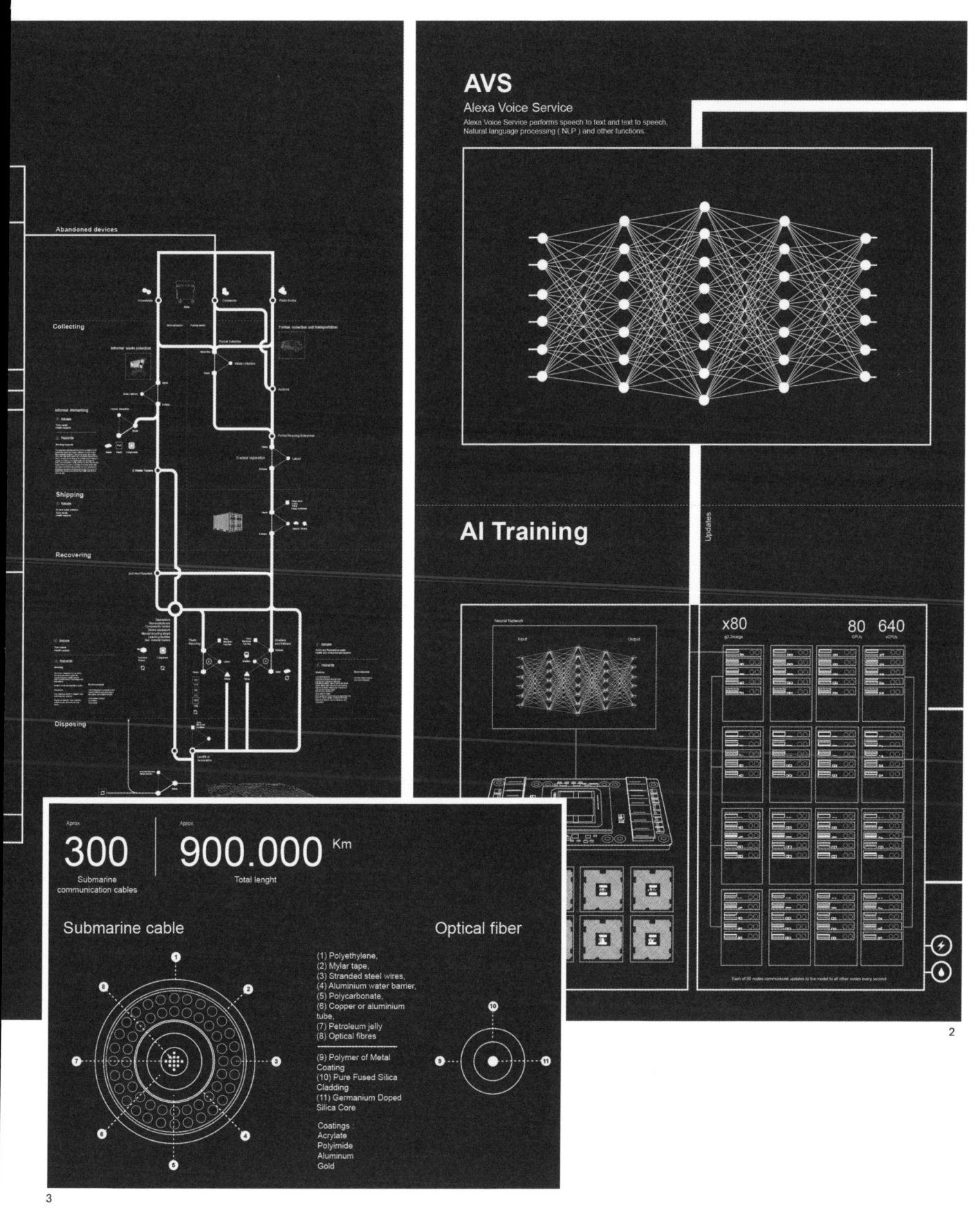

1 This diagram shows everything from the energy consumption of Amazon's storage centers to the geological process of extracting the rare earth elements and minerals required to create circuit boards and electric functions, as well as an estimated monthly salary in US dollars of everyone involved in the production chain.
2 A detail of how data is harvested en masse for training AI systems.
3 A detail of the submarine cables that carry data around the world.

Forensic Architecture, Eyal Weizman

Data is the raw material of a new frontier of architectural practice, often produced by social media, smartphones, CCTV footage, and satellites, as well as detailed metadata from weather-tracking software, AI, and machine learning. Forensic Architecture uses architectural techniques and technologies — such as highly accurate 3-D modeling and the construction of virtual reality environments — that apply this data to design in order to investigate human rights violations around the world. Led by architect Eyal Weizman, a professor of spatial and visual cultures at Goldsmiths, University of London, the agency consists of architects, artists, filmmakers, journalists, software developers, scientists, and lawyers, among others in an extended network. Storytelling is what makes the evidence compelling, along with synthetic images — photorealistic collages of Photoshopped images overlaid with data and 3-D models — the team can generate of contentious sites, such as spaces of war. Committed to developing and disseminating these new evidentiary techniques, Forensic Architecture works on behalf of international prosecutors, human rights organizations, and civil society groups, as well as political and environmental justice organizations.

1
1 Photographs and videos located within a 3-D model tell the story of one of the heaviest days of bombardment in the 2014 Israel-Gaza war.
2 Sea Watch versus the Libyan Coastguard. A rescue vessel operated by NGO Sea Watch en route toward a migrants' boat in distress in international waters on November 6, 2017.
3 A reconstruction of the search-and-rescue operations in the central Mediterranean.
4 An image projected onto a 3-D model in order to reconstruct the complicated scene.

207

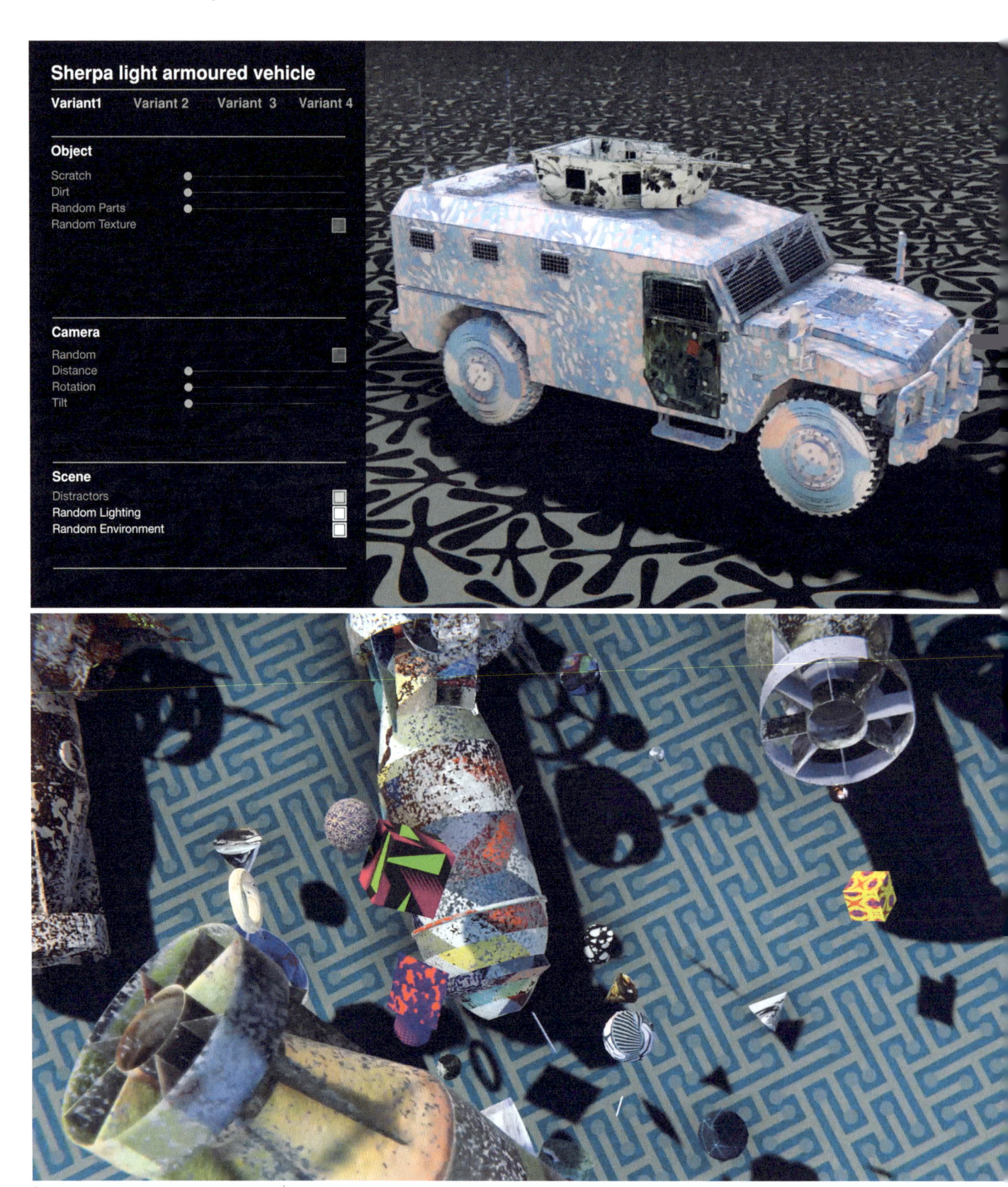

Forensic Architecture, Eyal Weizman

7

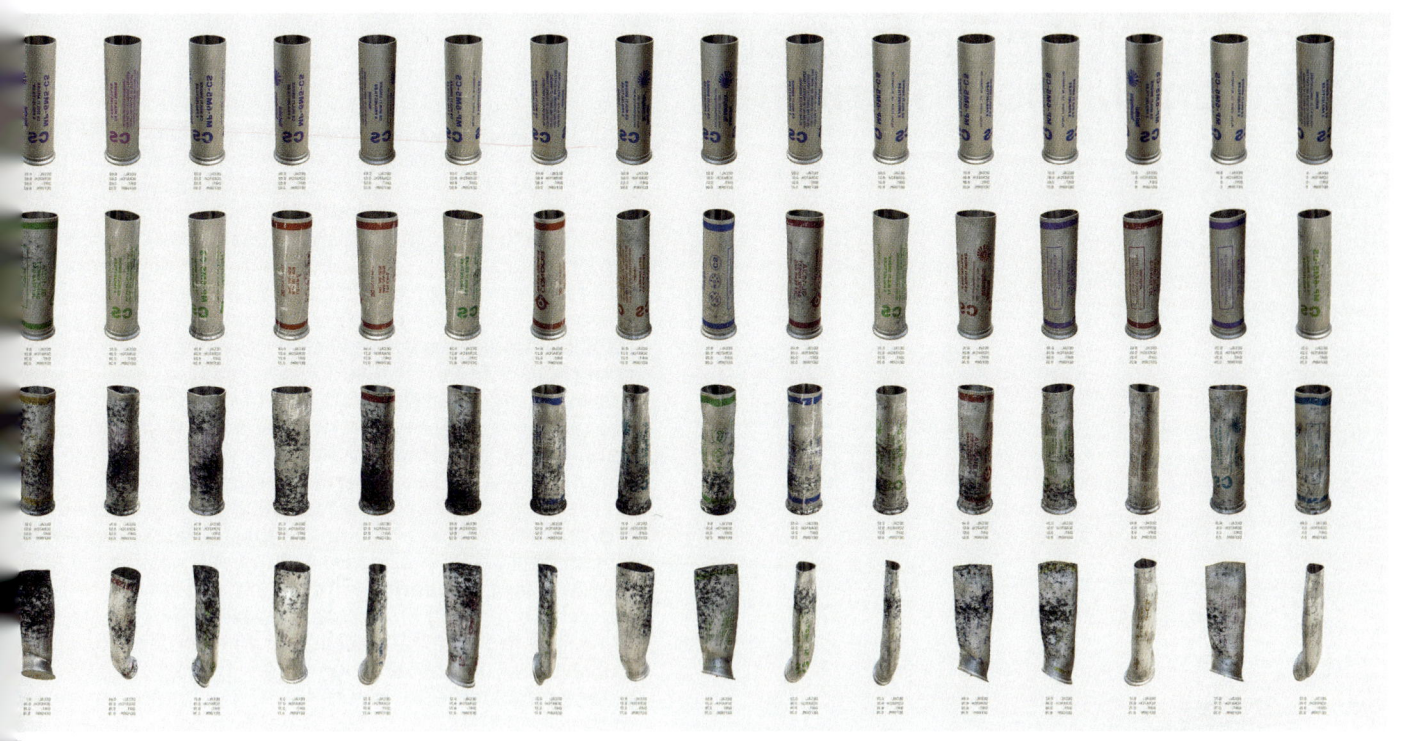

5   This rendered image of an armored vehicle textured with random patterns is an "extreme object," meaning it is unlikely to appear like this in a real-world scenario. However, machine learning classifiers that use rendered images of 3-D models or "synthetic data" are known to improve when trained using extreme variations of the modeled object.
6   By building a library of various 3-D modeled objects of violence, such as the M-4000 bomb shown here, the objects can be used to generate synthetic datasets with thousands of variations.
7   The 1.4 to 1.5 in. (37 to 40 mm) projectiles are some of the most common tear gas munitions deployed against protesters worldwide. The team is developing techniques to automate the search and identification of such projectiles among a huge number of videos online. Forensic Architecture modeled thousands of commonly found variations of this object, rendered them as images, and used these images as a way to train the machine learning classifier.
8   The team textured their modeled projectiles with random patterns. Such "extreme variations" help the classifier better recognize their shape, contours, and edges.

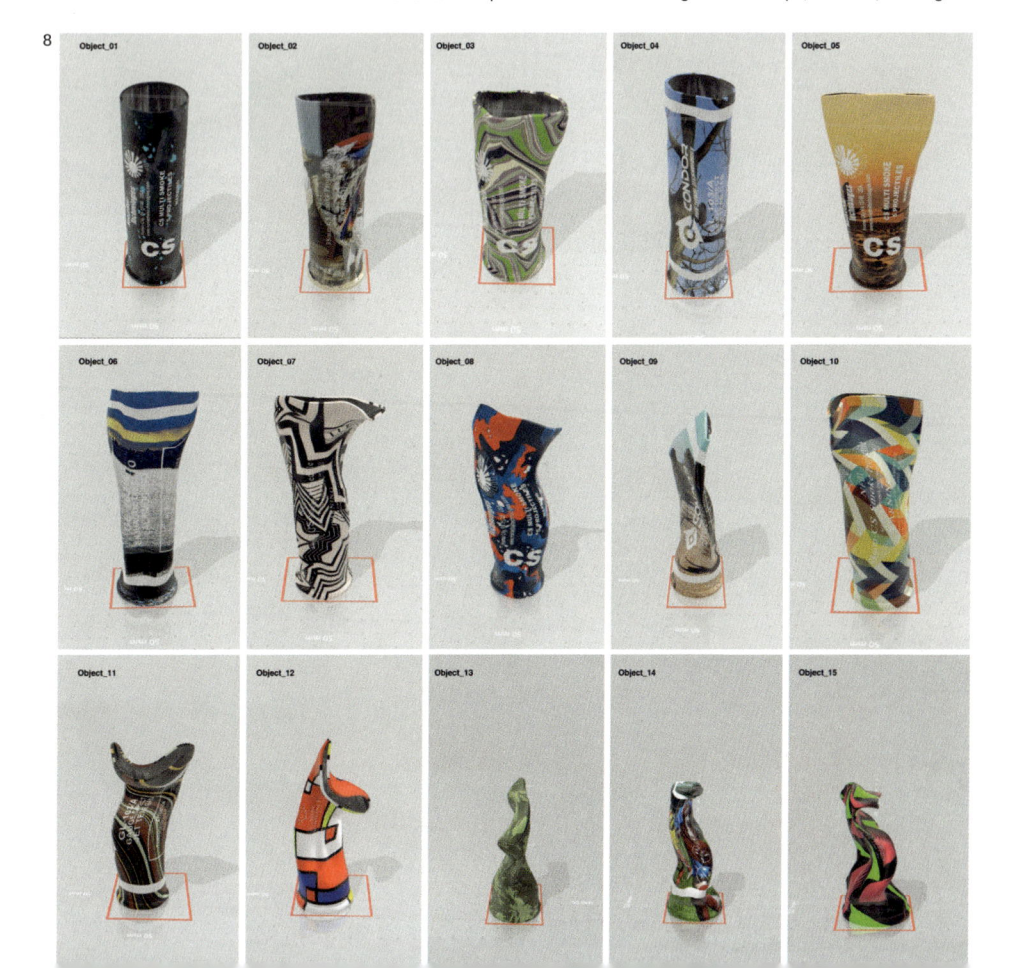

8

Masterminds   209

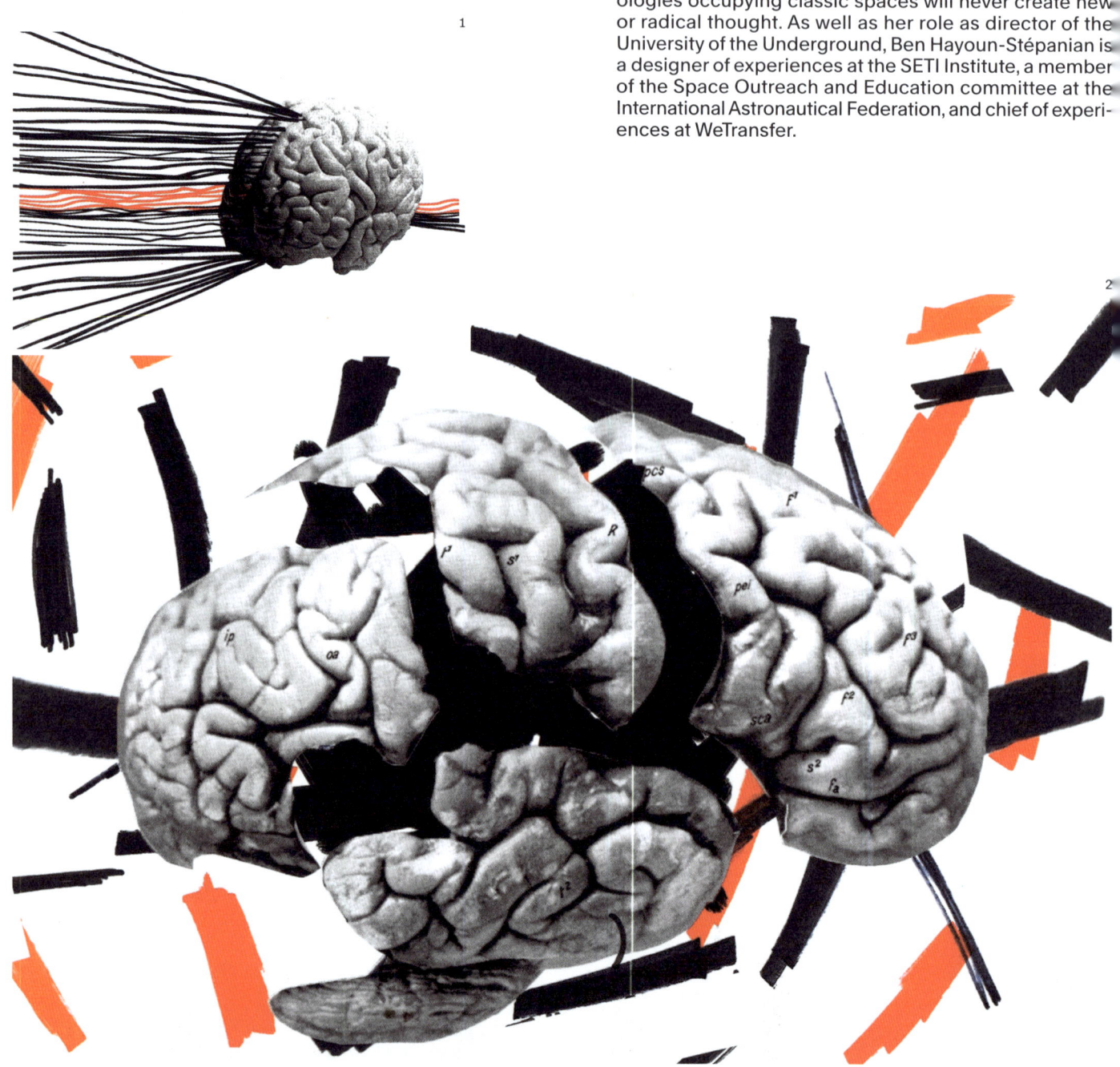

University of the Underground,
Nelly Ben Hayoun-Stépanian

London–based designer, educator, and filmmaker Nelly Ben Hayoun-Stépanian's practice is a pluralistic experiment — she constantly invents new ways to work, forging intellectual alliances with philosophers, astronauts, and even boxing clubs. In 2017 she founded the University of the Underground, an experimental, tuition-free university that teaches design activists and thinkers to ignite social change in institutions and governments. Its fittingly non-traditional locations are nightclub basements, with classes taking place in London and Amsterdam, as well as programs in Cairo and New York. With a passion for teaching design from a non-Western, nonhierarchical, and nonwhite perspective, Ben Hayoun-Stépanian cultivates counterculture by asking herself and her students what it would be like to teach from the perspective of a plant, for example, or from outer space. She established the program as a platform to encourage these pluralistic ways of thinking about design, arguing that traditional top-down methodologies occupying classic spaces will never create new or radical thought. As well as her role as director of the University of the Underground, Ben Hayoun-Stépanian is a designer of experiences at the SETI Institute, a member of the Space Outreach and Education committee at the International Astronautical Federation, and chief of experiences at WeTransfer.

3

1   This image forms part of the graphic identity for the University of the Underground, designed by Nelly Ben Hayoun Studios.
2   A brain is a recurring motif in the visual identity. Indeed, University of the Underground board members, activists, and great minds include Noam Chomsky, Nadya Tolokonnikova of Pussy Riot, and former MEP (Member of European Parliament) Magid Magid.
3   Interior view of the University of the Underground in Amsterdam, Netherlands.
4   The library at the University of the Underground in Amsterdam.

4

Masterminds   211

Bishan Commune, Ou Ning
Bishan, China, 2011–16

1   The 2011 Bishan harvest festival, curated by Ou Ning and his team, included outdoor screenings of Chinese movies.

Bishan Commune, Ou Ning
Bishan, China, 2011–16

In 2010 Chinese artist, curator, publisher, film director, and activist Ou Ning became fascinated by the fast-disappearing Chinese villages as a counterpoint to the country's extreme urban expansion. Between 2012 and 2016, he largely lived as part of the Bishan Commune, a small village of 2,600 people in Anhui Province. Inspired in part by an intellectual group that formed the rural reconstruction movement in China in the 1920s and the back-to-the-land movement in the 1960s and 1970s in North America, the Bishan Commune project began when Ou initiated a harvest festival in the village of Bishan in 2010, a monthlong event that included poetry classes, dance, contemporary art performances, and outdoor screenings of Chinese films, and an exhibition of photographs of village life before the commune. Ou and his family left their life in Beijing to live in a farmhouse in Bishan in 2012, subsequently founding a network of cultural projects, including a bookstore, a learning center, and an art gallery, as well as guesthouses. The commune took on many of the practices of utopian societies, including producing its own currency and passports. Despite the positive impact of tourism on the commune — employed to protect the rural ecology and lifestyle of the villagers — the project ultimately ended in 2016, as the central government sought to curtail the commune's autonomy and influence.

2   Completed in 2015, the School of Tillers — at the core of the project — often hosted artists' talks.
3   Pages from Ou Ning's notebooks, showing elements of his vision for the utopian microstate in the village of Bishan, China, including the design for a passport.

Masterminds

Duty Free Art, Hito Steyerl
2017

A visual artist, researcher, documentary filmmaker, academic, and essayist, Berlin–based Hito Steyerl systematically hones in on unexamined aspects of contemporary life, interrogating what passes as normal or moral, and offering critical thinking that traverses politics, cities, technology, war, aesthetics, philosophy, and the art world. In *Duty Free Art: Art in the Age of Planetary Civil War*, a collection of Steyerl's essays and talks, her observations present a mostly Western society that's filled with contradictions. In the book's title essay, Steyerl refers to the billions of dollars' worth of art that collectors keep in "free port" storage spaces, such as airports, which have no international territory and thus are not subject to tax. These collections, where a Picasso might share shelf space with a Damien Hirst, are a kind of hybrid of Amazon warehouse and world-class museum. Steyerl wants us to wonder if duty-free art is truly without duty, agency, and responsibility. Elsewhere, her cinematic installations blend documentary film techniques, speculative fiction, and first-person narrative, and are presented within immersive built environments.

1 Installation view of *Factory of the Sun*, 2016, MOCA Grand Avenue, Los Angeles. Hito Steyerl's immersive video work probes the pleasures and perils of image circulation in a moment defined by the unprecedented global flow of data.
2 Installation view of *Liquidity Inc.*, 2015, Artists Space, New York. In this thirty-minute video, Steyerl tells the story of a financial analyst who lost his job in the economic crash of 2008 and became a career mixed-martial-arts fighter.

Hyperobjects, Timothy Morton
2013

Philosopher and professor Timothy Morton has authored several transformative texts that reconstruct humankind's relationship to the planet. Morton has described their work as trying to "upgrade"[10] human beings to a state of ecological awareness, arguing that nature itself is an idea unhelpfully constructed by and for humanity. Even for those who want to protect it, nature is not a useful term, because it implies something separate from us, rather than encompassing us. For Morton, our species' survival depends on a symbiotic coexistence between humans, nonhuman animals, and the planet itself. They coined the term "hyperobjects" to describe hugely complex concepts whose magnitude makes them hard to fully grasp, such as global warming. The argument is that once something can be described, it can be addressed. It is estimated that Styrofoam could take up to a million years to fully degrade, so another hyperobject occupying vast amounts of time and space could be "all the Styrofoam in the world."[11] Morton's poetic and accessible proposition invites readers to use the term to find ways to think about some of the hardest to fathom phenomena in our contemporary world. For the artwork WE ARE THE ASTEROID, Morton collaborated with Brooklyn–based artist Justin Brice Guariglia in repurposing solar-powered LED traffic message boards to display phrases in reference to the climate crisis — the words of caution become literal warning signs.

1   Artist Justin Brice Guariglia's WE ARE THE ASTEROID I, 2018, with text by Timothy Morton, on display at Storm King Art Center in New Windsor, New York.
2   WE ARE THE ASTEROID II, 2018, on the Navy Pier in Chicago.
3   WE ARE THE ASTEROID I, 2018, on the grounds of Storm King Art Center.

Everything, David OReilly
2017

David OReilly is a multidisciplinary artist, animator, and filmmaker. *Everything* — part game, part philosophical experiment, part interactive nature documentary — allows players to assume the role of almost anything in the universe, from bacteria to a bear, starlings, planets, galaxies, or molecules. Traveling through the extraordinary game, a player discovers there are no rules or destinations, conflicts, or tasks; rather, the player begins to read and collect the thoughts of things, gradually generating these for herself or himself. For OReilly, while the game could nurture a deep reverence for the natural world, it is essentially taking an antienvironmental stance: positioning humans as interchangeable with other species, and identifying the interdependent biology that generates the planet. This is contrary to environmentalism, which positions the human species as dominating over nature. In reality, our imagination allows us to see variations of ourselves and our feelings in other humans and nonhuman animals, anthropomorphizing other species; yet the game offers an experience of radical empathy toward microcosms and inanimate materials, such as plants or pebbles, that would traditionally represent the boundary of our understanding. For OReilly, confronting these limits of human empathy and comprehension is a critical aspect of the experience.

1

1   Promotional artwork for the video game. The philosophical component of the project is heightened by the game's soundtrack, which is composed of a series of lectures by British philosopher Alan Watts.
2   The game allows players to imagine themselves as almost anything, including bears, from a micro to macro scale.
3   A pride of lions in *Everything*, rendered in David OReilly's signature low-polygonal aesthetic.
4   A bird's-eye view of the world as captured from the video game.

219

Stony Island Arts Bank, Theaster Gates
Chicago, IL, USA, 2017

1

US-born Theaster Gates is a leading example of artists as active protagonists and change agents in their cities. Following the purchase and restoration of a single dilapidated house on his block in South Chicago, Gates established the Rebuild Foundation, a nonprofit organization that acquires and renovates dozens of abandoned buildings and, in his words, "wakes them up,"[12] petitioning planners and city officials to allow change of use so that thriving cultural spaces can appear in formerly residential neighborhoods. The Rebuild Foundation is based on the core principles that Black people matter, Black spaces matter, and Black material objects matter, and in just a few years it has been responsible for the creation of an entirely new cultural district in Chicago, at the heart of which is the Stony Island Arts Bank. Gates bought the building, which had been empty for thirty years, for a dollar from the city and raised money to transform it into a library and archive of iconic Black magazines, including *Jet* and *Ebony*, as well as an exhibition space, a woodworking shop, and a place to talk about the complexities of race and class. That the Rebuild Foundation is thriving is in part due to its internal farm-to-table ethics that have established an ecosystem in which young people can learn construction and fabrication skills to renovate buildings themselves. Both labor and capital can be invested directly in the community, nourishing the foundation's fundamental goals.

1. A potent symbol for the Rebuild Foundation, the Stony Island Arts Bank is in a building with a commanding Classical Revival facade.
2. The former community bank and surrounding neighborhood fell into decline after the Great Depression.
3. The Johnson Publishing Archive & Collections room inside the restored Stony Island Arts Bank.
4. Before its transformation the building was utterly abandoned, and by the 1980s it was in a state of severe disrepair.

Dark Matter Labs, Indy Johar

1

Mapping the systems around childhood environment

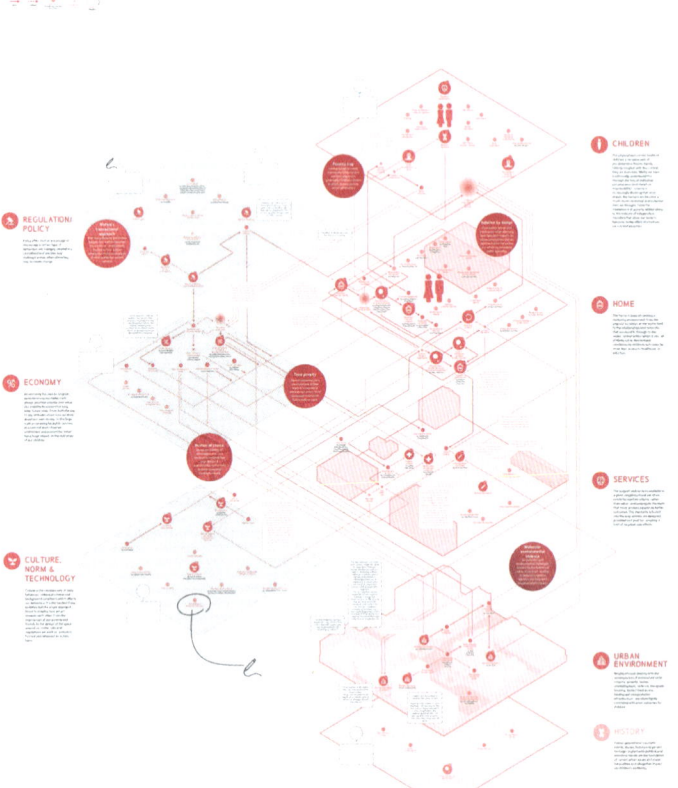

2

Future of Licensing

Future of Contracting

Future of Policy

Future of Rights

Dark Matter Labs

HACKABLE WARRANTIES

Each apartment, building or block could have a digital log of its materials, supply chain and construction process, monitoring performance where necessary. This could allow the creation of an 'aggregatable warranty', a single repository for tracking and proving upgrades and repairs. A new public platform could encourage people use, hack and recycle distributed and digitally manufactured building components and products, and incentivise a more circular use of materials.

Unlocking a local, circular economy

Dark Matter Labs

3

London–based design think tank Dark Matter Labs believes that architects need to develop new alliances and look beyond traditional design skills in order to enact substantial radical change. The studio maintains that the answers for how to create a more democratic, distributed, and ecologically responsible future are to design and develop a new kind of "dark matter" (the institutional infrastructure surrounding the creation of our built environment). According to founder Indy Johar, a global crisis of climate change and great social inequality can be understood as an exceedingly entangled and complex civic crisis, in which poverty is an institutionalized accepted consequence of exponential technological advancement and subsequent unchecked carbon emissions. An alternative world view, one that could solve this civic crisis, ensuring all production is inclusive of all life on our living planet, requires overhauling many conceptual frameworks, practices, and protocols. Collaborating with the likes of climate change think tanks, banks, and national and regional governments, the team develops strategies that encourage long-term thinking — for example, encouraging local municipalities to view trees as urban infrastructure and promoting the implementation of mass planting strategies, by delving into the way trees could be paid for, procured, and sustained.

1   Dark Matter Labs has been developing proposals for "radical childcare" in the UK, organizing committees to support innovative forms of learning through strategies including creating a "children's government," increasing diversity in early-years storybooks, and encouraging cities to invest in low-cost forms of public play.
2   This diagram shows a "full stack" of innovations that offer the possibility of radically distributing and democratizing how our cities are created and who creates them.
3   Blending Silicon Valley-style technology with every day civic needs, Dark Matter Labs proposed a system whereby housing components can be individually monitored, upgraded, repaired, or replaced.

The Transscalar Architecture of COVID-19, Ivan Lopez Munuera and Andrés Jaque
2020

The early weeks of the coronavirus pandemic came with an avalanche of never-before-seen images: from 3-D models of the novel virus to empty supermarkets and hastily constructed field hospitals. But the pandemic was not experienced in one universal way. This fourteen-minute film—commissioned for a public program in celebration of Earth Day in late April 2020—was influenced by Charles and Ray Eames's seminal film *Powers of Ten* (1977), which employed the system of exponentials to visualize scale, from the edges of the universe to the nucleus of an atom. New York–based scholar, critic, and curator Ivan L. Munuera collaborated with Andrés Jaque and the Office for Political Innovation to collate in detail the new data and spatial landscapes the coronavirus generated as it spread around the world. It was one of the first works of coronavirus culture, documenting the microbial details of the virus itself as it began to disseminate, along with socially distant encampments constructed for the homeless, mass graves, tracking apps, empty sports stadia, and near-deserted public spaces, as well as a diagram showing the reduction of carbon emissions in parallel with reduced plane traffic. The film underlines the entanglements between health, ecology, and economy, and highlights the cooperation, inventiveness, and emerging forms of togetherness that the human species found in this time of hardship.

1. The film documents deserted urban landscapes, as well as wild animals as they venture through the streets of desolate town centers.
2. While white-collar workers in developed societies worked from home, essential workers remained mobilized, raising questions of new bodied forms of inequality.

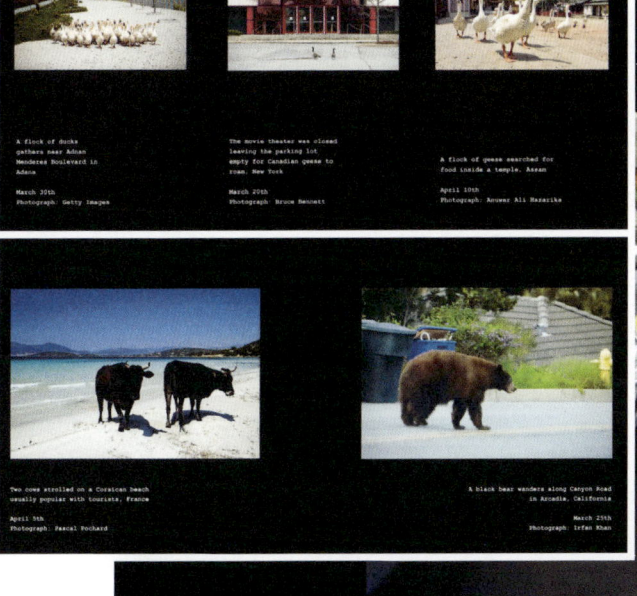

Space Enabled, Danielle Wood

1

Holistic, sustainable design doesn't stop at the limits of our planet. In space there are abundant opportunities too. Space Enabled, a research group based at the MIT Media Lab in Cambridge, Massachusetts, is led by Danielle Wood, who trained as an aerospace engineer and policy scholar. The group was founded in 2018 to research how designs enabled by space can also help advance environmental sustainability and justice on Earth. At the heart of Wood's motivation to develop these lateral-minded strategies is her realization that women of color around the world face major barriers in their pursuit of education, employment, and healthcare. Space Enabled Research Group, a community of scholars with expertise in a variety of fields — including geospatial analysis, artificial intelligence, social science, artistic practice, and equitable design — studies those issues at national and local scale. Within Space Enabled, Prathima Muniyappa is collaborating with the Khasi people of northeastern India to preserve ancient knowledge of the use of tree roots to create bridges; Ufuoma Ovienmhada uses data from satellites, aerial vehicles, and water sensors to create online maps of an invasive plant in Benin, working with a local company to convert the plant into a product that absorbs oil-based waste; while Juliet Wanyiri is examining ways that rocket fuel might be sustainable if it were based on non-toxic ingredients, such as candlewax and beeswax.

1   Researcher Ufuoma Ovienmhada flying an aerial vehicle to map coastal mangrove forests and invasive plants to support environmental management in the republic of Benin.

Space Enabled, Danielle Wood

2
3

226

4

2   An image from the 2018 installation *Earthrise: A 50 Year Contemplation*. This Space Enabled project sought to inspire concern for the care of planet Earth.
3   Space Enabled researcher Juliet Wanyiri (right) works with retired NASA astronaut Catherine Coleman to study the use of candlewax as potential fuel for satellites.
4   An image from NASA's LandSat series showing crop circles in Kansas farms. Space Enabled often uses data about the environment to inform policy makers.
5   Researcher Prathima Muniyappa designs approaches to cultural conservation in collaboration with the Khasi people of Meghalaya state in northeastern India. "As a Khasi, our lives are intricately linked to the preservation of our traditional practice of building living architecture … Our root bridges are a reminder of ancient routes through a valley green and our age-old ability to blend our human needs in harmony with nature." — MorningStar Khongthaw.[13]

5

Masterminds

Further Reading

Amale Andraos and Nora Akawi, eds., *The Arab City: Architecture and Representation* (New York: Columbia University Press, 2016)
Academics and architects Amale Andraos and Nora Akawi collaborated on this insightful work exploring contemporary and historic architectural production in the Middle East, seeking to dismantle stereotypes of the region. In a series of essays, the book covers the vast scope of regional differences, and the specificities of its architectural and urban canons. Contributors include practitioners from Design Earth and Forensic Architecture as well as academic leaders such as Mabel O. Wilson, Adrian Lahoud, and Hashim Sarkis.

Paola Antonelli, *Broken Nature: Design Takes on Human Survival (Triennale di Milano)* (Milan: Mondadori Electa, 2019)
Paola Antonelli is senior curator of Architecture and Design and founding director of Research and Development at the Museum of Modern Art in New York. Her expansive and investigative approach to curating combines design, architecture, art, science, and technology. The catalogue for her 2019 exhibition *Broken Nature* for the XXII Triennale di Milano examines the threads that connect humans to their natural environments. In exploring objects and concepts of all scales, and in all materials, it celebrates design's ability to offer powerful insight into key issues of our age.

Shumon Basar, Douglas Coupland, and Hans Ulrich Obrist, *The Age of Earthquakes: A Guide to the Extreme Present* (New York: Blue Rider Press, 2015)
Part contribution to meme culture, part profound cultural analysis, *The Age of Earthquakes* is inspired by Canadian philosopher Marshall McLuhan's groundbreaking book *The Medium is the Massage: An Inventory of Effects*, which looked at the influence of technology on contemporary culture. Shumon Basar, Douglas Coupland, and Hans Ulrich Obrist extend McLuhan's now fifty-year-old analysis up to today through a provocative blending of text and image.

Irene Cheng, Mabel O. Wilson, and Charles L. Davis II, eds., *Race and Modern Architecture: A Critical History from the Enlightenment to the Present* (Pittsburgh: University of Pittsburgh Press, 2020)
The story of race and racism is permanently written into architectural history in this important publication. Taking their lead from the intersection of slavery, colonialism, and inequality, the editors analyze the key concepts of Modernism against the social realities of the time and question the much-accepted premise that the movement was a force for social equality by showing how race played a major role in establishing and reaffirming Modernist ideals.

Beatriz Colomina and Mark Wigley, *Are We Human?: Notes on an Archaeology of Design* (Zürich: Lars Müller, 2017)
For the 2016 Istanbul Design Biennial, Beatriz Colomina and Mark Wigley asked the question: Are we human? A runthrough of ideas covering everything from the efforts of our prehistoric ancestors to develop a sense of self through cave painting and in shaping tools from stone, to the interconnected online self of today, this book and the exhibition of the same name cover hundreds of thousands of years of design history.

Caroline Criado-Perez, *Invisible Women: Exposing Data Bias in a World Designed for Men* (New York: Harry N. Abrams, 2019)
Caroline Criado-Perez made her name as the campaigner for British banknotes to feature the image of Jane Austen. In this book she uncovers the heavily biased role of data in reaffirming existing structural sexism in the design industry. Her research explores the previously uncritical reliance many designers have on algorithms that are skewed toward male bodies and male research subjects. The resulting bias and discrimination shines an uncomfortable light on the lack of representation and consideration for female bodies in almost every aspect of society — from the way snow is usually cleared from roads onto sidewalks, making walking with strollers more hazardous, to how car safety uses an average height and weight of male bodies to design the location of the seat-belt and airbag, meaning that women are 47 percent more likely to be injured in a car accident than men.

Arturo Escobar, *Designs for the Pluriverse: Radical Interdependence, Autonomy, and the Making of Worlds* (Durham, NC: Duke University Press, 2018)
In this book, Colombian academic Arturo Escobar presents the history of design from the perspective of the global south, and its multifaceted crisis of poverty, inequality, and climate. Escobar considers much of design as a way to reinforce existing political systems to produce consumer goods or digital services, and suggests that instead designers could create many interdependent worlds — a pluriverse of futures — that address different aspects of human experience, considering the rights of indigenous communities in designing environments and wider decolonizing efforts across Latin American cities.

LaToya Ruby Frazier, *The Notion of Family* (New York: Aperture, 2014)
An intimate and tender portrait of a family and a great introduction to the thinking and practice of artist, photographer, activist, and advocate LaToya Ruby Frazier. *The Notion of Family* situates Frazier's grandmother Ruby alongside herself and her mother as three generations of Black women in the predominantly working-class Rust Belt town of Braddock, Pennsylvania. Through duotone images and color video stills, the work also documents Frazier's own struggles and interactions with her family and community.

Rania Ghosn and El Hadi Jazairy, *Geostories: Another Architecture for the Environment* (Barcelona: Actar, 2018)
Rania Ghosn and El Hadi Jazairy are founding partners of the practice Design Earth, which explores aesthetic forms of environmental engagement. This is a collection of fantastical architectural ideas and illustrations that are part cli-fi (climate fiction) and part Victorian-era etching, that together offer ideas for and reflections on the absurdity of solving the current ecological crisis on earth. From oil extraction to deep-sea mining, air pollution, and space debris, *Geostories* provides futuristic macro-level analysis of the dream-like ways in which societies may survive, thrive, and exist in the decades and centuries ahead.

Mario Gooden, *Dark Space: Architecture, Representation, Black Identity* (New York: Columbia University Press, 2016)
This collection of five essays by architect Mario Gooden investigates how planning, building, and pre-existing expectations of how public space can be used have all been intimately involved in the construction of African American identity. Gooden interrogates symbols of a universalized African experience, such as kente cloth or masks, which have been used in cultural institutional settings, and discusses ways to philosophize the more complex issues of heritage in the African diaspora.

Sandi Hilal, Alessandro Petti, and Eyal Weizman, *Architecture After Revolution* (Berlin: Sternberg Press, 2013)
From their base in Palestine, the architectural collective Decolonizing Architecture Art Research (DAAR) focus their work on speculations, educational programs, and spatial interventions. This publication comprises a series of fictional architectural stories set in different locations across Palestine that poetically and provocatively imagine the morning after a revolution. Their notion of struggles for equality from the perspective of displaced refugees offers an important perspective different from that of the concerned liberal Western citizen.

María Puig de la Bellacasa, *Matters of Care: Speculative Ethics in More Than Human Worlds* (Minneapolis: University of Minnesota Press, 2017)
The notion of care has been considerably gendered, but in a current climate in which governmental politics and policies are becoming deliberately incendiary and often discriminatory, many architects and designers are growing more interested in the politics of caring and empathy as a design tool. *Matters of Care* takes cues from Donna Haraway, Judith Butler, and Bruno Latour in its distillation and analysis of non-anthropocentric ways of relating to and caring for life on Earth.

Kate Raworth, *Doughnut Economics* (Hartford, VT: Chelsea Green Publishing, 2018)
In 2019 English economist Kate Raworth drew a diagram consisting of two concentric rings that showed her vision of a sustainable economic future in the hall of the United Nations in New York, NY. Her revolutionary *Doughnut Economics* model proposes a new way to think about cycles of growth and suggests ways to design economies that better suit the genuine needs of communities and countries — rather than growing for growth's sake. Her model argues that human life can only survive in a safety zone where both social needs and environmental concerns are met. She asks: "How can we turn economies that need to grow, whether or not they make us thrive, into economies that make us thrive, whether or not they grow?"

Alice Rawsthorn, *Hello World: Where Design Meets Life* (New York: Penguin, 2013)
From her position as one of the world's preeminent design critics, Alice Rawsthorn provides an essential read that spans the history of the field, sharing expansive and ambitious definitions as she traverses the design of everything from neighborhoods through to typefaces.

Marwa al-Sabouni, *The Battle for Home: Memoir of a Syrian Architect* (London: Thames & Hudson, 2017)
Marwa al-Sabouni's memoir on her experience as an architect living and working in the midst of the Syrian civil war made a huge impact when it was published. Her eyewitness account from Homs explores the breakdown of society, from the destruction of churches and mosques to the corruption of officials involved in planning. She includes her own hand-drawn sketches of the destruction as well as proposals for social housing projects to solve the desperate situation in her war-torn city.

Anna Lowenhaupt Tsing, *The Mushroom at the End of the World: On the Possibility of Life in Capitalist Ruins* (Princeton, NJ: Princeton University Press, 2017)
In this book, Anna Tsing takes readers on a journey to learn about the world's most valuable mushroom, in the process creating a modern parable about the human species' impact on the rest of life on earth. The matsutake is both a highly expensive Japanese delicacy and a generative fungus that supports the growth of trees in greatly damaged landscapes. In revealing the connections between the forest's survival and the unimaginable desirability of a mushroom, Tsing discovers unexpected nuances of capitalism and ecology.

Chris Ware, *Building Stories* (New York: Pantheon Books, 2012)
Building Stories is part art object, part dynamic architectural drawing, and part comic book. Redefining the genre of the graphic novel, the finished work is a box that contains fourteen different publications varying in materiality and scale. The images include brightly colored sectional diagrams that tenderly reveal snatches of the lives of four occupants of a three-story Chicago apartment building.

Liam Young, *Machine Landscapes: Architectures of the Post Anthropocene* (Hoboken, NJ: Wiley, 2019)
Filmmaker and academic Liam Young devotes much of his career to understanding the near future. In this collection of essays and observations, Young explores the architectural spaces of today: data centers, distribution warehouses, and unmanned ports that are designed for and filled with server stacks and hard drives, instead of people. Young explores the epoch of the Anthropocene and proposes that the post-Anthropocene will be occupied by these sinister new typologies of non-human-centered design.

Shoshana Zuboff, *The Age of Surveillance Capitalism* (New York: PublicAffairs, 2019)
Harvard professor Shoshana Zuboff coined the phrase *surveillance capitalism* to describe a darkly familiar phenomenon that she argues could be responsible for the wholesale transformation of human nature in the twenty-first century. In this book, she tracks the vast concentrations of behavioral data gathered by Silicon Valley and subsequent sales of that information to "behavioral" futures markets that create goods and services that are then sold to modify and control such behavior. Zuboff explores the consequences of this to democracies, freedom, and the future of our species.

Index

Page numbers in *italics* refer to illustrations

Adeyemi, Kunlé 26
Adjaye, Sir David 68
Adjaye Associates, National Museum of African American History and Culture 66–9, *68*
Aerial Domesticity, Mexico City 28, *28*, *29*
AI Now Institute 204, *204–5*
Aichi Triennale, Nagoya (2019) 198
Albers, Josef 42
Amager Resource Center, Copenhagen (CopenHill) 94, *94–9*
Amateur Architecture Studio, Fuyang Cultural Complex 76–7, *77*
Amazon *204–5*, 216
    Amazon Alexa 204
    Amazon Echo 204
Amazon rain forest 156
American Red Cross 15
Ando, Tadao, Church of the Light 169
Ando, Yoko 101
Antarctica 54, *55*, 56
anti-Brexit campaign 142–3, *143*
Aravena, Alejandro 70
Archizoom, No-Stop City 180
Art Biotop Water Garden, Nasu *86–9*
Artists Space, New York 216
Asia One 140, *140–1*
Assemble, Granby Four Streets 176, *176*
Atelier Masōmī, Hikma Religious and Secular Complex 160–3, *160*
Aymara people 31

Bait Ur Rouf Mosque, Dhaka 90, *90–3*
Bamboo Hostels, Baoxi 188, *188–91*
Barragán, Luis 128, *128*
Beachler, Hannah, *Black Panther* 146–7, *147*
Beartooth Portal, Fishtail, MT 183, *185*
Bêka, Ila
    Moriyama-San 130, *130–3*
Ben Hayoun-Stépanian, Nelly, University of the Underground 210, *210–11*
Benítez, Solanito 22
Benítez, Solano 22
BIG, CopenHill 94, *94–9*
Bishan Commune *212–15*, 214
Bishan Harvest Festival *212–13*
Black Lives Matter 145, 147
Black Panther 146–7, *147*
Boeri, Stefano 120
Bofill, Ricardo, La Fábrica 154
Bosco Verticale 120

Brexit referendum 143
Bridle, James, *New Dark Age: Technology and the End of the Future* 198, *198*
Britain Stronger in Europe campaign 143
Broid, Isaac 115
Burj Khalifa, Dubai *56–7*

Cabral, Gloria 22
Cadalso, Eleanna 28
Caizhai village, China 165
Cao Fei, *Asia One* 140, *140–1*
Carnic Alps, Italy 120
Carson, Anne 104
Casa Barragán, Mexico City 128
Central Park, Taichung 36, *36–9*
Century of Progress International Exposition (1934) 201
Chapel in Guastalla 177, *177*
Cho, Minsuk 45
Choi, Jae-Eun 45
Cité du Grand Parc, Paris 111
Classical Revival 220–1
CLIMAVORE: On Tidal Zones 52, *52–3*
Cobb family 136
Colomina, Beatriz, *X-Ray Architecture* 200, *200–1*
Color(ed) Theory, Chicago 42, *42–3*
Community Farm, Englewood 186, *187*
Constructivism 129
Cooking Sections, CLIMAVORE: On Tidal Zones 52, *52–3*
CopenHill, Copenhagen 94, *94–9*
Craigslist 28
Crawford, Kate
    AI Now Institute 204, *204–5*
    Anatomy of an AI System 204
"Critical Water Security Plan" 56
Crow, Jim 49
Crown Royal 42
Crystal House, Century of Progress International Exposition 201

Dana, Karine, *The Imaginaries of Transformation* 110–11, 111
Dark Matter Labs 222, *222*
A Dead Forest for the Trojan Women, Syracuse 120, *120–1*
Deeterink Rooftiles 46
Design Earth, *Of Oil and Ice* 54–7, *55*
Design Museum, London, *Fear and Love* exhibition (2016) 24
Dignitas 34–5, *35*
Diller Scofidio + Renfro, the *Mile-Long Opera* 102–5, *104*
DMZ Vault of Life and Knowledge 44–5, *45*

DnA_Design and Architecture, A Songyang Story 164, *164–7*
Domo, Fishtail, MT *182–3*, 183
Donna Haraway: Story Telling for Earthly Survival 202, *202–3*
Drawing Architecture Studio, Taobao Village — Smallacre City 180, *180–1*
Druot, Frédéric, *The Imaginaries of Transformation* 110–11, 111
Dushan leisure center, Songyang 165
Duty Free Art: Art in the Age of Planetary Civil War 216, *216*

Eames, Charles and Ray, *Powers of Ten* 223
Earth Day 223
Earthrise: A 50 Year Contemplation 226
Elemental, Ocho Quebradas House 70, *70–3*
Emergent Vernacular Architecture, Tapis Rouge 14–15, *15*
Ensamble Studio, Structures of Landscape *182–5*, 183
Escobedo, Frida, Serpentine Pavilion 168, *168*
Esmaili, Yasaman 160
Euripides, *The Trojan Women* 120
Everything 218, *218–19*

Factory of the Sun 216
Fear and Love exhibition, Design Museum, London (2016) 24
Feedlots 124, *124–7*
Flat House, Cambridgeshire 178, *178–9*
Flint Is Family Part I 136, *136–9*
Floyd, George 80
Fondation Cartier pour l'art contemporain, Paris, France 156
Forensic Architecture 206, *206–9*
Frazier, LaToya Ruby 136, *136–9*
A Friend 150, *150–1*
Furness, Avril, *The Last Moments* 34–5, *35*
Futurism 129
Fuyang Cultural Complex 76–7, *77*

Gabinete de Arquitectura, Quincho Tía Coral 22, *22–3*
Game of Drones. Of Unmanned Aerial Vehicles exhibition (2019), Zeppelin Museum 198
Gang, Jeanne 80
Garfield Park Conservatory, Chicago 174, *174–5*
Gates, Theaster, Stony Island Arts Bank 220, *220–1*

Gaza Strip 83
Gerrard, John, *Western Flag (Spindletop, Texas) 2017* 134, *134–5*
Ghana Cocoa Board 150
Ghosn, Rania 55
Global Communities 15
Go Hasegawa, chapel in Guastalla 177, *177*
Goldsmiths, University of London 206
Granby Four Streets, Liverpool 176, *176*
Granby Four Streets Community Land Trust 176
Granby Winter Garden 176
Grand Parc Bordeaux, France *110–11*
The Great Animal Orchestra 156, *156–7*
Great Depression (1929–33) 221
Great Mosque of Samarra, Iraq 56–7
Grindr 24
Guariglia, Justin Brice 217
  We Are the Asteroid 217

Hadid, Zaha 147
Haiek, Alejandro 28
happn 25
Haraway, Donna
  Staying with the Trouble: Making Kin in the Chthulucene 202
Heatherwick, Thomas 61
Heatherwick Studio, Zeitz MOCCA 60–3, *61*
Heneghan Peng, Palestinian Museum 82–3, *83*
Hengken village, China 165
Henner, Mishka 124, *124–7*
Heringer, Anna, Bamboo Hostels 188, *188–91*
Herzog & de Meuron 192
High Line, New York 104
Hikma Religious and Secular Complex, Dandaji 160, *160–3*
Hirst, Damien 216
Hormuz Dam, the Gulf 55, *56, 57*
Houses of Parliament, London 144
Housing+, Ciudad Acuña 112, *112–13*
HOWL, eon (I, II) 129, *129*
Hurricane Katrina (2005) 145
Hurricane Sandy Rebuilding Task Force 94
hyperobjects 217, *217*

The Imaginaries of Transformation 110–11, *111*
In the Robot Skies 40–1, *41*
Ingels, Bjarke 94
Institute for Contemporary Art, Ljubljana 198

The Institute of Isolation 152–5, *154*
International Architecture Exhibition of the Venice Biennale (2018) 169
International Astronautical Federation 210
International Bamboo Architecture Biennale 188, *188–91*
Intimate Strangers 24, *24, 25*
Inverted Portal, Fishtail, MT 183
The invisible enemy should not exist 144, *144*
Iquique 70
Ishigami, Junya 88
Islamic State 144
Israel–Gaza war (2014) 206

Jafa, Arthur, *Love is the Message, The Message is Death* 145, *145*
James, LeBron 145
Jaque, Andrés 223
  The Transscalar Architecture of COVID-19 223, *223*
  Intimate Strangers 24, *24, 25*
Jazairy, El Hadi 55
Johar, Indy, Dark Matter Labs 222, *222*
Johnson Publishing Archive & Collections 221
Joler, Vladan, AI Now Institute 204, *204–5*
Juaçaba, Carla, Vatican Chapel 169, *169*
Junya Ishigami + Associates, Art Biotop Water Garden 86–9

Kahiu, Wanuri, *Rafiki* 199
Kamara, Mariam 160
Kazuyo Sejima + Associates, Laview Commuter Train *100–1*, 101
Keck, George Fred, Crystal House *201*
Kéré Architecture, Lycée Schorge 74–7, *75*
Kéré, Francis 75
Khasi people *227*
Koolhaas, Rem 130
  CCTV tower 140
Krausas, Veronika, *De Aere (concerning the air)* 174
Krause, Bernie, *The Great Animal Orchestra* 156, *156–7*
Kurokawa, Kisho, Agricultural City 180

Lab.Pro.Fab, *Aerial Domesticity* 28, *28, 29*
Lacaton, Anne 111
Lacaton & Vassal, *The Imaginaries of Transformation* 110–11, *111*
L'air pour l'ai, Chicago 174, *174–5*

Lake County Tuberculosis Sanatorium *200*
lamassu 144, *144*
Lang, David 104
The Last Moments 34–5, *35*
Latour, Bruno 204
Laview Commuter Train *100–1*, 101
Le Corbusier 42, 200
Lemoine, Louise
  Moriyama-San 130, *130–3*
Leonidov, Ivan, Magnitogorsk 180
Libyan Coastguard *207*
Liquidity Inc 216
Loos, Adolf 200
Love is the Message, The Message is Death 145, *145*
Lucas gusher, Texas 134
Lycée Schorge, Gando 74–7, *75*

McQueen, Steve, *Year 3* 148, *148–9*
McRae, Lucy, *The Institute of Isolation* 152–5, *154*
Magid, Jill, *The Proposal* 128, *128*
Mahama, Ibrahim, *A Friend* 150, *150–1*
Makoko Floating School, Lagos Lagoon 26, *26–7*
Mamani, Freddy, New Andean Architecture 30–3, *31*
March on Washington for Jobs and Freedom (1963) 145
Marching Cobras of New York 48, *48–51*
Marching On 48, *48–51*
Marcus Garvey Park, New York City *48–9*
Margent Farm, Cambridgeshire 178
Marvel 147
MASS Studies, DMZ Vault of Life and Knowledge 44–5, *45*
Material Cultures 178
Matta-Clark, Gordon 61
Maughan, Tim 41
Meghalaya state, India *227*
Mehretu, Julie, HOWL, eon (I, II) 129, *129*
Mesoamerican civilization 115
Miami Museum Garage 192, *192–5*
Mies van der Rohe, Ludwig 200
Mile-Long Opera, New York 102–5, *104*
MIT, Cambridge, MA 225
MOCA Grand Avenue, Los Angeles 216
Modernism 128, 150, 200
Mori, Toshiko, THREAD: Artists' Residency and Cultural Center 106–9, *107*
Moriyama, Yasuo 130, *130–3*
Moriyama-San 130, *130–3*

Radical Architecture of the Future   233

Morton, Timothy *217*
 Hyperobjects 217, *217*
Mugatsia, Samantha 199
Muharraq, Bahrain, Pearling Site Museum and entrance 116–19, *117*
Munuera, Ivan Lopez, *The Transscalar Architecture of COVID-19* 223, *223*
Munyiva, Sheila 199
Museum of Modern Art, New York 204

National Geographic 55
National Museum of African American History and Culture, Washington 66–9, *68*
NAVE, Santiago 64, *64–5*
Navy Pier, Chicago *217*
Nelly Ben Hayoun Studio, University of the Underground 210, *210–11*
Nergal Gate of Nineveh 144
New Andean Architecture, El Alto 30–3, *31*
New Dark Age: Technology and the End of the Future 198, *198*
Nishizawa, Ryue, Moriyama House 130, *130–3*
NLÉ, Makoko Floating School 26, *26–7*
North Korea 45

Obama, Barack 145
Ocho Quebradas House, Los Vilos 70, *70–3*
Of Oil and Ice 54–7, *55*
Office for Political Innovation 223
 Intimate Strangers 24, *24*, *25*
Olgiati, Valerio, Pearling Site Museum and entrance 116–19, *117*
OMA 192
Opalis 46, *46–7*
OReilly, David, *Everything* 218, *218–19*
Ou Ning, Bishan Commune 212–15, *214*

Palestinian Museum, Birzeit 82–5, *83*
Pearling Site Museum and entrance, Muharraq 116–19, *117*
Performa 17 48
Philippe Rahm architectes, Central Park 36, *36–9*
Picasso, Pablo 216
Pingtian village, China *166*
Plasencia Auditorium and Congress Center, Spain 16–21, *19*
Polis Station, Chicago 80, *80–1*
Porta Venezia, Milan 150, *150–1*
Portal, Fishtail, MT *184*

Practice Architecture, Flat House 178, *178–9*
Pratt, Emmanuel 186
Price, Cedric 64
Productora, Teopanzolco Cultural Center 114–15, *115*
The Proposal 128, *128*
Prvački, Ana 174
Punchdrunk 35

Quincho Tía Coral, Asunción 22, *22–3*

Radić, Smiljan, NAVE 64, *64–5*
Rafah, Gaza *206*
Rafiki 199
Rahm, Philippe 36
Rakowitz, Michael, *The invisible enemy should not exist* 144, *144*
Rankine, Claudia 104
Rebuild Foundation 220, *220–1*
redlining 186
Regenerative Neighborhood Development, Chicago 186, *186–7*
Revista Nacional de Arquitectura 126 200
Riley, Terence 192
Roberts, Bryony, *Marching On* 48, *48–51*
Rossi, Aldo 64
Rotor DC, Opalis 46, *46–7*
Royal Academy of Arts, London 143
Royal Botanic Gardens, Kew, London 154, *154*

San Giorgio Maggiore, Venice 169
SANAA 101, 130
School of Tillers, Bishan *214–15*
Sea Watch 207
Second Life 140
Seibu Railway company 100–1, *101*
Sejima, Kazuyo 101
SelgasCano, Plasencia Auditorium and Congress Center 16–19, *19*
Sennacherib 144
Serpentine Pavilion, London 168, *168*
SETI (Search for Extraterrestrial Intelligence) Institute 210
Shimen Bridge *167*
Smithsonian Institution 68
SO—IL, *L'air pour l'ai* 174, *174–5*
Somerset House, London Edmond J. Safra Fountain Court *142–3*
A Songyang Story, Songyang 164, *164–7*
Space Enabled 224–6, *225*
 Earthrise: A 50 Year Contemplation 226

Stefano Boeri Architetti, A Dead Forest for the Trojan Women 120, *120–1*
Steinbeck Studios 176
Steiner, Rudolf 36
Steyerl, Hito, *Duty Free Art: Art in the Age of Planetary Civil War* 216, *216*
Stony Island Arts Bank, Chicago 220, *220–1*
Storefront for Art and Architecture, New York City 48
Storm King Art Center, New Windsor, NY *217*
Storm Vaia (2018) 120, *120*
Strait of Hormuz Dam 57
Structures of Landscape, Fishtail, MT 182–5, *183*
Studio Chahar, Hikma Religious and Secular Complex 160–3, *160*
Studio Gang, Polis Station 80, *80–1*
Sweet Water Foundation, Regenerative Neighborhood Development 186, *186–7*

Taawon 83
Tabassum, Marina, Bait Ur Rouf Mosque 90, *90–3*
Taobao Village—Smallacre City 180, *180–1*
Tapis Rouge, Port-au-Prince 14–15, *15*
Tate Britain, London 148
Teatro Greco 120
TEN Arquitectos 192
Teopanzolco Cultural Center, Cuernavaca 114–15, *115*
Terranova, Fabrizio, *Donna Haraway: Story Telling for Earthly Survival* 202, *202–3*
THREAD: Artists' Residency and Cultural Center, Sinthian 106–9, *107*
Tillmans, Wolfgang, *Pro-EU / Anti-Brexit Campaign* 142–3, *143*
Tinder 25
Tippet Rise Art Center, Fishtail, MT 182–5, *183*
Torzo, Francesca, Z33 new wing 170, *170–3*
Toyota 94
The Transscalar Architecture of COVID-19 223, *223*
Turner Prize 143, 176

Uganda 147
Ultra Sheen 42
UNESCO 116–19, 188
United Visual Artists, *The Great Animal Orchestra* 156, *156–7*

University of the Underground
 210, *210-11*
Unknown Fields Division 41

Vassal, Jean-Philippe 111
Vatican Chapel, Venice 169, *169*
Vatican City 169
Vertical Forest 120
Vitra 128

Watts, Alan *218*
Weizman, Eyal, Forensic Architecture
 206, *206-9*
West, Kanye 145
West Bank 83
Western Flag (Spindletop, Texas) 2017
 134, *134-5*
Williams, Amanda, *Color(ed) Theory*
 42, *42-3*
Wilson, Mabel O., *Marching On*
 48, *48-51*
Wood, Danielle, Space Enabled
 224-6, 225
WORKac, Miami Museum Garage
 192, *192-5*
Wright, Frank Lloyd, Broadacre City
 180

X-ray 200
X-Ray Architecture 200, *200-1*
Xu Tiantian 164

Year 3 148, *148-9*
Young, Liam, *In the Robot Skies*
 40-1, 41

Z33 House for Contemporary Art,
 Design and Architecture, Hasselt
 170, *170-3*
Zeitz MOCCA, Cape Town *60-3*, 61
Zeppelin Museum, Friedrichshafen
 198
Zumthor, Peter 170

Radical Architecture of the Future

Image Credits

14: © Gianluca Stefani
15: © Clément Davy
16–21: © Iwan Baan
22–23: © Federico Cairoli
24–25: © Andrés Jaque / Office for Political Innovation
26: © Iwan Baan
27: © NLÉ
28–29: © LabProFab. Additional project contributors: Heini Hölsenbaud, Armando Quintana, and Irina Urriola
30–33: © Peter Granser. From the book *El Alto* published by Edition Taube
34–35: © Avril Furness
36–39: Courtesy of Philippe Rahm architectes
40–41: © Liam Young
42–43: © Amanda Williams
44–45: © Minsuk Cho/Mass Studies
47: © Rotor
48, 49, 50 (t), 51 (t): © Jenica Heintzelman
50 (b), 51 (b): © Bryony Roberts
52: Photo: Ruth Clark
53 (t): Photo: Cooking Sections
53 (b): Photo: Nick Middleton
54–57: © Design Earth
60–62: © Iwan Baan
63: © Hufton + Crow
64–65: © Cristobal Palma
66–69: © Alan Karchmer/NMAAHC
70–72: © Cristobal Palma
73 (t): Courtesy of Alejandro Aravena
74 (b): Courtesy of Elemental
74–77: © Iwan Baan
78–79: © Iwan Baan
81 (b): © Spirit of Space
80, 81 (t): © Studio Gang
82–85: © Iwan Baan
86–87: © junya.ishigami + associates
88 (l): Courtesy of nikissimo Inc.
88 (r), 89: © junya.ishigami + associates
90–93: © Marina Tabassum Architects
94, 98 (t): © Laurian Ghinitoiu
95, 96–97, 98 (b), 99: © Rasmus Hjortshoj
100–101: © Kazuyo Sejima & Associates
102–103: © Timothy Schenck
104, 105: © Iwan Baan
106–109: Photos: Iwan Baan. Courtesy of Toshiko Mori Architect
110–11: © Philippe Ruault
112–13: Photos: Jaime Navarro
114–15: Photos: Onnis Luque
116–19: © Archive Olgiati
120: Tempesta Vaia. Courtesy of Regione Veneto
121: Stefano Boeri Architetti, Un Bosco Morto, Le Troiane Siracusa
124–27: © Mishka Henner
128 (t): Image: Stefan Jaeggi, Kunst Halle Sankt Gallen, 2016. Courtesy of the artist and LABOR, Mexico City
128 (b): Courtesy of the artist, Field of Vision, and Oscilloscope Laboratories

129: Photo: Tom Powel Imaging. Courtesy of Julie Mehretu and Marian Goodman Gallery
130–33: © Bêka & Lemoine
134, 135 (t): © John Gerrard
135 (b): © John Gerrard. Photo: Somerset House
136–39: © Courtesy of LaToya Ruby Frazier and Gavin Brown's enterprise, New York and Rome
140–41: Courtesy of Cao Fei, Vitamin Creative Space, and Sprüth Magers
142: Jeff Spicer/Stringer
143: Photos: Wolfgang Tillmans/Between Bridges
144: Commissioned for the Mayor of London's Fourth Plinth Programme. Courtesy of the Mayor of London. Photos: Caroline Teo and Gautier Deblonde
145 (t): Courtesy of the Museum of Contemporary Art, Los Angeles. Photo: Brian Forrest
145 (b): Courtesy of Arthur Jafa and Gavin Brown's enterprise, New York/Rome
146–47: © Marvel Studios
148–149: Steve McQueen, Year 3. A partnership between Tate, Artangel, and A New Direction. © Steve McQueen & Tate. Courtesy of Artangel. Billboards photographed in situ by Theo Christelis.
150–51: Installation view at Caselli Daziari Porta Venezia, Milan 2019/Courtesy of Fondazione Nicola Trussardi, Milan/Photo: Marco De Scalzi
152–53: Photo: Daniel Gower
154: © Lucy McRae
155: Photos: Lotje Sodderland
156: Photo: Luc Boegly
157: Photos: James Medcraft
160–63: © James Wang. Courtesy of Atelier Masōmī and Studio Chahar
164–67: Photos: Wang Ziling
168: © Rafael Gamo
169: © Federico Cairoli
170–73: © Gion Balthasar von Albertini
174–75: © Iwan Baan
176: Courtesy of Assemble
177: © Stefano Graziani
178–79: © Oskar Proctor
180–81: © Drawing Architecture Studio
182–85: © Iwan Baan
186–87: ©Sweet Water Foundation
188–89, 191: © Julien Lanoo
190: Courtesy of Anna Heringer
192–95: © ImagenSubliminal (Miguel de Guzman + Rocio Romero)
198: © James Bridle
199: © Big World Cinema/Afrobubblegum
200: Revista Nacional de Arquitectura, vol.126, June 1952. Official body of the Higher Council of the Spanish Architects' Association. Published by the Colegio Oficial de Arquitectos de Madrid
201 (t): *Le Visage de l'enfance* (Paris: Horizon, 1937) 212
201 (b): HB-09789-A. Chicago History Museum, Hedrich-Blessing Collection
202–203: © Graphoui/Fabrizio Terra nova/CBA
204–205: © Kate Crawford and Vladan Joler

206–209: © Forensic Architecture
210: © Nelly Ben Hayoun Studios
211: Photos: Gianfranco Tripodo
212–13: Photos: Hu Xiaogeng
214: Photo: Zhu Rui
215: © Ou Ning
216 (t): Courtesy of Hito Steyerl, Andrew Kreps Gallery, New York, and Esther Schipper, Berlin. Installation view, Hito Steyerl, Artists Space, New York, March 8–May 24, 2015. © Matthew Septimus
216 (b): Courtesy of Hito Steyerl, Andrew Kreps Gallery, New York, and Esther Schipper, Berlin. Installation view of Hito Steyerl: Factory of the Sun, February 21–September 12, 2016 at MOCA Grand Avenue, courtesy of the Museum of Contemporary Art, Los Angeles. Photo: Justin Lubliner
217: © The Studio of Justin Brice Guariglia and Maruani Mercier Gallery
218–19: © David OReilly
220, 221 (b): Photos: Sara Pooley
221 (m): © Steve Hall
222: © Dark Matter Labs
223: © Andrés Jaque and Ivan L. Munuera with the Office for Political Innovation
224–25: Photo: David Lagomasino. Project contributors: Fohla Mouftaou, Lola Fatoyinbo, David Lagomasino, and Danielle Wood
226 (t): Project contributors: Lizbeth B. de la Torre, Rachel Petersen, Frank White, Katlyn Turner, Jonathan Wood, and Danielle Wood
226 (b): Photo: Steve Boxall
227 (t): Image: NASA
227 (b): Photo: Prathima Muniyappa
Front cover image: Photo: Luc Boegly
Back cover image: © Andrés Jaque / Office for Political Innovation

Every reasonable effort has been made to acknowledge the ownership of copyright for images included in this volume. Any errors that may have occurred are inadvertent and will be corrected in subsequent editions provided notification is sent in writing to the publisher.

Endnotes

Architecture's Radical Future

1. Beatrice Galilee held the inaugural position of Daniel Brodsky Associate Curator of Architecture and Design from 2014 to 2019.
2. Arturo Escobar, "Introduction: Finding Pluriversal Paths." In Ashish Kothari, Ariel Salleh, Arturo Escobar, Federico Demaria, and Alberto Acosta, eds, *Pluriverse: A Post-Development Dictionary* (New Delhi: Tulika Books, 2019) xxi.
3. Donna Haraway, "A Cyborg Manifesto: Science, Technology, and Socialist-Feminism in the Late Twentieth Century." In *Simians, Cyborgs and Women: The Reinvention of Nature* (New York: Routledge, 1991) 179.
4. "Pizol glacier: Swiss hold funeral for ice lost to global warming," BBC, September 22, 2019, www.bbc.com/news/world-europe-49788483.
5. Marlowe Hood, "'Warning to humanity': Stop killing insects now before it's too late, say scientists," *Science Alert*, February 11, 2020, www.sciencealert.com/half-a-million-insect-species-face-extinction-and-we-re-doing-nothing-about-it.
6. Katherine Dunn, "Oil prices go negative for the first time in history," *Fortune*, April 20, 2020, www.fortune.com/2020/04/20/oil-prices-negative-crash-price-crude-market.
7. Magdalena Petrova and Andrew Ross Sorkin, "This 13-foot robot cost over $100 million to develop and looks like it's straight out of a sci-fi movie," CNBC, March 3, 2020, www.cnbc.com/2018/03/01/hankook-miraes-sci-fi-looking-robot-cost-over-100-million-to-develop.html.
8. Harm Venhuizen, "AOC proposes measure to put an end to military recruiting using esports teams, livestreaming," *Military Times*, July 23, 2020, www.militarytimes.com/news/your-army/2020/07/23/aoc-proposes-measure-to-put-an-end-to-military-recruiting-using-esports-teams-livestreaming.
9. Paola Antonelli, *Broken Nature: Design Takes on Human Survival* (New York: Rizzoli Electa, 2019) 40.
10. Beatriz Colomina and Mark Wigley, *Are We Human? Notes on an Archaeology of Design* (Zürich: Lars Müller Publishers, 2016) 71.
11. Bernard Rudofsky, *Architecture Without Architects: A Short Introduction to Non-Pedigreed Architecture* (1964; reprinted Albuquerque: University of New Mexico Press, 1987) 1.
12. In the global south, many are still fighting for the autonomy of their countries' resources, as Uruguayan historian Eduardo Galeano's work was dedicated to unravelling. In his book *Open Veins of Latin America* (1973; reprinted New York: Monthly Review Press, 1971) 2 he wrote: "Latin America is the region of open veins. Everything, from the discovery until our times, has always been transmuted into European — or later United States — capital, and as such has accumulated on distant centers of power. Everything: the soil, its fruits and its mineral-rich depths, the people and their capacity to work and to consume, natural resources and human resources."
13. Another prominent female architect at this time was the British-born Modernist Jane Drew. Female critics and theorists, such as Ada Louise Huxtable, Jane Jacobs, and Denise Scott Brown, also held significant positions in public discourse.
14. The exhibition involved using 3-D scanning to replicate one hundred objects from the Metropolitan Museum of Art's collection, fusing them with facsimiles of contemporary human figures. The sixteen sculptures were rendered in the same black or white polyurethane and coated in a thin layer of dust, giving the impression that the humans, now petrified, had been caught mid-play with these liberated objects.

Project Texts

1. Avril Furness, lecture. *In Our Time: A Year of Architecture in a Day* symposium. Metropolitan Museum of Art, New York, NY, December 9, 2017.
2. Alejandro Aravena, as quoted in "Alejandro Aravena: the shape of things to come," *Guardian*, April 10, 2016, www.theguardian.com/artanddesign/2016/apr/10/architect-alejandro-aravena-pritzker-prize-elemental-housing-iquique-constitucion-tsunami-defences.
3. Tatiana Bilbao, "A House is Not Just a House," *Architect* magazine, October 17, 2018, www.architectmagazine.com/design/a-house-is-not-just-a-house_o.
4. See for instance Cao Fei's photo series *COSPlayers* (2004).
5. Michael Rakowitz, as quoted in "Latest Trafalgar Square Fourth plinth artwork unveiled," BBC, March 28, 2018, www.bbc.co.uk/news/uk-england-london-43565870.
6. For example, materials that use plastics, have chemical coatings, or require training to install.
7. Niall McCarthy, "China used more concrete in 3 years than the U.S. used in the entire 20th century," *Forbes*, December 5, 2014, www.forbes.com/sites/niallmccarthy/2014/12/05/china-used-more-concrete-in-3-years-than-the-u-s-used-in-the-entire-20th-century-infographic/#29fd9c894131.
8. James Bridle, lecture. *In Our Time: A Year of Architecture in a Day* symposium. Metropolitan Museum of Art, New York, NY, January 19, 2019.
9. Wanuri Kahiu, "We need a new image of Africa." World Economic Forum, March 15, 2018, www.youtube.com/watch?v=JMODpgDU6jQ.
10. Timothy Morton, "Introducing the idea of 'hyperobjects,'" *High Country News*, January 19, 2015, www.hcn.org/issues/47.1/introducing-the-idea-of-hyperobjects
11. Morton, *Hyperobjects: Philosophy and Ecology after the End of the World* (Minneapolis: University of Minnesota Press, 2013) 60.
12. Theaster Gates, "How to revive a neighborhood: with imagination, beauty and art." *TED: Ideas Worth Spreading*, March 2015, www.ted.com/talks/theaster_gates_how_to_revive_a_neighborhood_with_imagination_beauty_and_art/transcript.
13. The Khasi people of Meghalaya state in northeastern India worked closely with Space Enabled Lab, informing their approach to cultural conservation: "As a Khasi, our lives are intricately linked to the preservation of our traditional practice of building living architecture as a solution for the modern world. Our root bridges are our history, a reminder of ancient routes through a valley green and our age-old ability to blend our human needs in harmony with nature." — MorningStar Khongthaw.